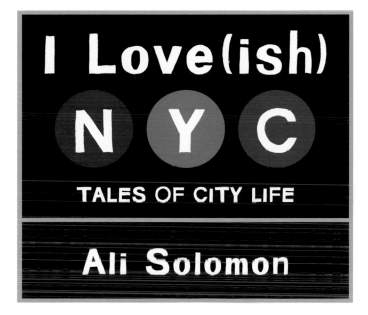

I Love(ish) NYC

TALES OF CITY LIFE

Ali Solomon

CHRONICLE BOOKS

SAN FRANCISCO

To Marla & Marty Solomon, the OG New Yorkers,
whose stories about their childhoods made New York
sound both thrilling and terrifying.

"Oddly Specific NYC Neighborhoods" was co-created with Janine Annett. "Apartment Optical Illusions" first appeared on newyorker.com on February 8, 2021. "A Giving Tree Grows in Brooklyn" first appeared on mcsweeneys. net on January 22, 2020. "Millennial Math Problems" first appeared on medium.com/slackjaw on April 5, 2018.

Library of Congress Cataloging-in-Publication Data is available.

ISBN 978-1-7972-1655-3

Manufactured in China.

Design by Jon Glick

10 9 8 7 6 5 4 3 2 1

Chronicle books and gifts are available at special quantity discounts to corporations, professional associations, literacy programs, and other organizations. For details and discount information, please contact our premiums department at corporatesales@chroniclebooks.com or at 1-800-759-0190.

Chronicle Books LLC
680 Second Street
San Francisco, California 94107
www.chroniclebooks.com

CONTENTS

Prologue:
Life Cycle of
a New Yorker

Growing up in a suburb of Manhattan, I'd always regarded the city with a sense of awe and fear. Sure, it housed a humongous dinosaur skeleton, a 100% man-made park filled with 100% man-made ducks, and an overpriced, morally confusing musical about a phantom that haunts an opera house. But the city was also the place where both my parents were mugged, the family car was stolen, and those folks on "Law & Order" constantly stumbled across dead bodies in alleyways.

Naturally, I moved to the city and have lived here for the past twenty years.

There are times when I want to call it a day and hightail it to a place where I don't need to sidestep around feces every morning. A place where I won't pay two-thirds of my salary for one-third of an apartment. Where I won't have to wedge myself into a jam-packed train car and stand indefinitely while it figures out how to uncross its signals.

But then I remember that it's been more than a decade since I've been to a mall or gotten behind the wheel of a car, and it's glorious. That my neighbor was a Broadway dancer, my dry cleaner's daughter is running for local office, and everyone speaks more languages than I do. It's the kind of place where I'd go to the theater asking for tickets to see *The Mask*, and they'd assume I meant the German silent film from the 1930s. Where I can order Thai food from the good place, the *other* good place, or the *really* good place, all located three minutes from my doorstep. That at any moment I can do anything, anywhere, or nothing at all.

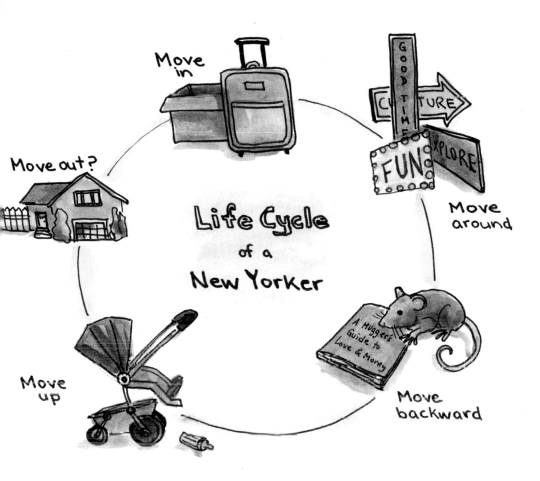

I'll eventually move out of the city. You know, "for the kids." Or for more storage for my books. Or to be closer to family that in terms of mileage aren't that far, but the George Washington Bridge might as well be the width of the Outback. But it won't be easy to shake. I'll be at a barbecue in someone's backyard, and while the kids mangle themselves on a trampoline, a PTA mom will ask me where I'm from. And no matter what suburb I've landed in, or which state I currently call home, my answer will always be the same:

"I'm from New York."

Stage 1: Laying the Eggs

There are a myriad of ways you've arrived here, the greatest city in the world:

Your parents grew up in the Bronx and raised you in Westchester, but you're curious about all this "Arthur Avenue" chatter.

You decided to attend NYU because you hear it has a "strong liberal arts program" and offers in-state tuition (probably, right?).

Your family emigrated from Argentina to Hell's Kitchen without skipping a beat.

You realize all the jobs you applied for are within a six-block radius of lower Manhattan.

You were born and raised in Bay Ridge and will probably marry the boy next door and eventually die there (and be buried by Parry & Sons Funeral Home — you went to grade school with all three Parry boys).

Whatever the method, **welcome!**

Stage 2: Larva

You've lived in New York City long enough to feel a sense of comfort. Look at you, using muscle memory to navigate the web of subways and buses to get anywhere in forty minutes! Impressive, timing your GrubHub order so your sushi is waiting for you just as you reach your apartment. Well done — your job is entry-level but pays benefits, you have three weeks of vacation that you waste on a house-share in Amagansett, and the local bartenders all know your order (Stoli & 7) and have it sitting on the bar by 6:30 p.m. every Thursday night, like clockwork.

You love your apartment even though it's really just a tiny, sweaty concrete box above a laundromat. You've painted an accent wall and lofted your bed above your kitchenette, which also doubles as your closet and bathroom.

Stage 3: Pupa

You're really living it up now. You make enough money to rent a one-bedroom apartment in a neighborhood within six blocks of a train, with laundry in the basement and an elevator. Occasionally you splurge on an Uber, you no longer purchase all your clothes at the T.J. Maxx in Midtown, and you don't even flinch when the waitress takes away your twenty-five-dollar glass of zinfandel before you've finished the last sip.

Your partner moves in with you, and your apartment has just enough space that you don't break up immediately. You talk about what pets your building allows. You prefer to see star-studded plays over splashy musicals and sign up for TodayTix because you can never commit to a show months in advance. The time has come for you to finally outgrow jazz clubs, improv comedy, and every restaurant in Union Square, but you still find upscale pizza places "charming."

You now get five weeks of vacation that you waste attending the weddings of your out-of-state college friends.

Stage 4: Adult

Everyone in your neighborhood knows you as the crazy lady who got her double-stroller stuck in a revolving door at Whole Foods. Your one-bedroom apartment feels much more cramped now that you've converted your linen closet into a nursery for your twins and your bedroom into a rec center, but you own it, and the mortgage is paid for by the bonus that came with your promotion, which ironically keeps you from spending any time in your apartment. You walk everywhere (mostly because of that semitrailer-sized stroller) and marvel at how much you love your neighborhood, while not having time to enjoy it whatsoever. The local bartender knows your drink order (club soda to help remove the small ketchup handprints on the back of your sweater), FreshDirect bags are your new form of luggage, and you spend a lot of time researching the stats of the local elementary schools.

You get six weeks of vacation from your job (or as they call it, "maternity leave"), but it doesn't really feel like time off because time has no meaning anymore, you know?

You wonder if it's too late in life to take an improv class.

Your mom keeps emailing you Zillow listings, but you love your neighborhood so much and would never dream of abandoning the city for the blandness of a four-bedroom house with radiant heating in the bathroom, superwide sidewalks, and the ability for your children to attend a high school just because they live nearby.

Would you?

Stage 5: Butterfly?

There are any number of ways you can move forward with your life: You can put down roots and declare your urban enclave your forever home, learn to live with less stuff, and spend a lot of time dragging your family on neighborhood adventures. Or you could drift over a bridge or through a tunnel and wind up in a slightly roomier apartment in a marginally more spread-out neighborhood with perhaps a few more trees and a local playground. Or you can uproot your family to a brand-new town or state (Google searches: "Affordable towns New Jersey," "Why is everyone moving to North Carolina?" "What is radiant heating?").

Whatever you decide, be it laying your eggs on the same leaf or spreading your wings and flying away without getting hit by a bus, the city will always be here, in case you want to visit.

You'll totally visit, right?

Stage 6: Laying Eggs Again

Wait, your daughter wants to go to NYU? Jesus. Doesn't she know how expensive it is to live in the city?

At least, when you drop her off for orientation, you'll get to go to that gourmet pizza place again. You wonder if it still has the butternut squash and burrata slice.

1

START SPREADING THE NEWS

Preparing for the Big Move

So, you've decided the place for you to live at this stage of your life is New York City. Maybe you've just graduated from college and have high hopes of landing a coveted position in some creative field – perhaps writing for one of those dying embers called a "magazine." Or your job transfers you from your native Philly to somewhere on Wall Street, and you see the move as a placeholder until your life course-corrects. Perhaps you've lived forever on the suburban outskirts, a bridge-and-tunneler who finally gets to trade in her flat iron for the Flatiron. Or maybe you're back to clean out your parents' co-op in Inwood after they decamp to Florida.

Either way, you can't just show up to New York expecting a warm hug and affordable rent. You need a plan.

Look for an Apartment

This will take you anywhere from three hours to three years. Show up to every apartment viewing with a blank check in your hand, zero expectations, and enough cash in the bank to fund a year of living dangerously. Be prepared to act quickly, fight off the hordes of grad students looking for something "sorta near Washington Square," and settle for any space that doesn't resemble a crime scene. Remember that scene in *Big* when Tom Hanks flees his home and winds up in a depressing city hotel, but in the next scene moves into that spacious pad with the bunk bed and all the toys? Right now you're not looking for your fun zone, you're searching for your flophouse.

Get Your Passport in Order

You may be thinking "But New York City is in the United States!" Or "I haven't used the darn thing since spring break senior year," or "I don't know where my birth certificate is!" All these things are accurate, but no self-respecting denizen of NYC travels sans passport. You never know if your job will transfer you overseas, or if your apartment's pipes will freeze in February and it's cheaper to fly to Mexico for a week than to fix them, or if you'll leave your wallet in the back of your Lyft and need ID to get past security at Condé Nast.

Change Your Address

On everything – your driver's license, the aforementioned passport, tax forms, job records. If you keep any of your old addresses on things, be prepared to receive six simultaneous jury summons, all in the different counties you've formerly lived.

Change Your Name

You only need to do this if you've stolen money from your previous employer and are looking to restart your life under a false identity.

Find a New Bank

Luckily, there's one on every street corner. Sometimes more than one!

Get Packing

Now is the time to purge stuff you don't need, like your prom dress, more than two towels, Playbills from every show you've seen since 2002, and your ironic T-shirt collection (make sure you save one with your alma mater on it to wear for job interviews). Do you need to bring an umbrella? Yes. It's not Seattle, but it definitely rains in New York, usually minutes after you've had your hair blown out, or when you plan a picnic in Central Park. Bring shoes good for walking, running, and dodging pedestrians who insist on checking their phones in the middle of the sidewalk. Pack all your favorite books and that copy of *The Goldfinch*, because you will definitely finally start it now.

And don't forget your phone charger again.

Watch a Lot of Unrealistic TV Shows Set in NYC to Prepare for Your New Life

Television is a mirror into our lives. Whether you're one of the six people who watched *Gossip Girl* and thought, "I had a debutante ball just like that!", believed *Sex and the City* implied you could freelance and also afford shoes not made from rubber, or you're convinced that *The Deuce* was written about your uncle, NYC is never more realistic than on the small screen.

Even when it's just a soundstage in Vancouver.

Advice Your Parents Gave You When You Moved to the City

(Based on New York City Movies They Saw in the 1970s)

"Try to travel in a group, so if you encounter a gang in the park late at night, you can take them on."

"No matter how fast you drive, you can never outrun a train."

"Taxi drivers will bend over backward to
make sure you get home safely."

"Now honey, we never saw the movie, but we
hear the streets are really mean."

"If you find yourself in a hostage situation, fake a heart attack
or seizure or something. Then you'll be released first!"

"When you go out dancing at the discotheques,
make sure you pick a nice partner."

"I don't care how many Broadway marquees
they added, Times Square is a shithole."

Newcomer Bucket List

Here's a list of things every New Yorker needs to do before they die or move away. If you don't accomplish at least three-quarters of the things on this list, were you even here?

1. **Meet an attractive stranger** on the observation deck of the Empire State Building. Ask him for the time.

2. **Visit all five boroughs** in one exciting night of transit fun.

3. **Take selfies with all the still-living celebrities** in Madame Tussauds, then tell your friends you met them at Balthazar.

4. **Ride the Cyclone in Coney Island**. Then take a yellow cab over the Queensboro Bridge during rush hour. Which was scarier?

5. **Take the Staten Island Ferry** for great views of the Statue of Liberty, and the Statue of Liberty Ferry for great views of Staten Island.

6. **Visit the dinosaur exhibit** at the Museum of Natural History, the Egyptian exhibit at the Metropolitan Museum of Art, and the Hall of Red Dots and Squiggles at the MoMA.

7. **Discover a body** in Central Park.

8. **Take a romantic horse-and-carriage ride** through Central Park. See if the driver will wait for you while you pick up your dry cleaning, grab takeout, and rob a local bank.

9. **Wait in a long line** for tickets to see Channing Tatum star as Titus Andronicus at the Delacorte Theater.

10. **Walk across the Brooklyn Bridge** at sunrise. Try not to get hit by a cyclist or drop your phone into the East River while taking your requisite selfie.

11. **Take the ferry to Governors Island** and repeatedly ask people where the prison is located.

12. **Run at least one New York City Marathon.** Afterwards, visit at least one New York City physiotherapist.

13. **Visit Times Square** on New Year's Eve, wind up peeing in an empty Gatorade bottle while 80,000 strangers try to kiss you.

14. **Attend the tree lighting ceremony** at Rockefeller Center, wind up peeing in an empty hot chocolate cup while 80,000 strangers try to hug you.

15. **Buy tickets to the Radio City Christmas Spectacular,** then resell them for 200 times the face value. Only in New York!

16. **Travel the length of the Highline,** a public park converted from an abandoned freight rail. Then check out the North Brooklyn Pipeline, a former park that is turning into a fracking machine.

17. **Eat yourself into a stupor** at Smorgasburg Williamsburg, then spend the next few hours filling your giant pineapple drink with disgust and regret.

18. **Hit on a man in uniform during Fleet Week**, even if you don't know when that is exactly, and the only uniformed person around is your mail carrier.

19. **Stop by Squiffy's**, order the Peaky Blinder (whiskey, Twinings tea, and Worcester sauce), and participate in their famous Wednesday night Trivia and Axe Throwing Competition.

20. **Eat in every restaurant** at least once. Except the TGI Fridays in lower Manhattan.

21. **Attend an improv show.** Ask the bearded ticket-checker why there are so many Ss in ASSSSCAT.

22. **Try to figure out** what everyone is waiting in line for.

23. **Go to a Moth show** and get pissed when a teenager with some fishy story about a childhood car accident gets picked instead of you.

24. **Wear a Red Sox jersey** to a Yankees game, just to stir shit up.

25. **Buy an "I Heart N.Y." T-shirt** from a gift shop near Port Authority and mail it to your mom so she, too, can feel like a real New Yorker.

You Are Here

27

". . . and from this room, you have a view
of a much nicer apartment."

2

FINDING YOUR DREAM APARTMENT, TRYING TO DRIVE OUT ITS CURRENT OCCUPANTS BEETLEJUICE-STYLE, THEN ULTIMATELY MOVING IN WITH A WORK ACQUAINTANCE AND HER SEVEN ROOMMATES

Apartment
Optical Illusions

1. The Infinite Walk-up

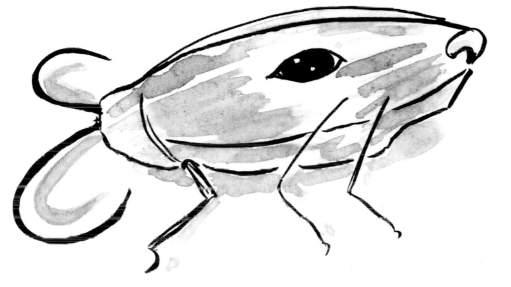

2. Do you see a mouse or a gigantic cockroach emerging from your stove? Is it possible you see both?

3. Put together your new IKEA desk without any help. For the next decade, take this desk with you every time you move, despite its being completely nonfunctional.

4. You and your roommate are both on the lease and pay the same amount in rent and utilities. Why does her room seem so much bigger than yours?

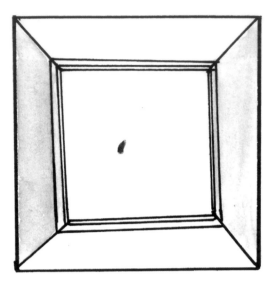

5. Stare at the brown dot on your ceiling for thirty seconds. Then look at a blank wall. Did the brown dot multiply? Are the dots moving?

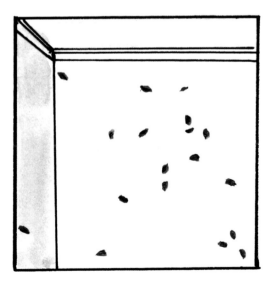

6. Is the water stain on your bathroom ceiling
yellow and white, or blue and black?

7. Did your secondhand bed come with three slats or four? Do you realize yet that it needs five slats to keep the mattress from sagging in the middle?

8. Which is at a shorter distance?

a. Your radiator, which sounds as if a grenade exploded inside a steel drum.

b. Your only window, which has the insulation capacity of a damp tissue.

9. You finally found a new roommate. Which one do you see?

a. Kayla, a twenty-four-year-old sociology grad student acquaintance who's willing to split her studio apartment with you, as long as you have a full-year's rent in cash, upfront.

b. Your great-aunt Sandy in the Bronx, who has a second bedroom, enough cat dander to coat both your lungs, and every issue of *Time* from 1968 onward.

10. Which shade of smoker's-lung gray will your landlord paint the apartment, four years after you've moved out? Will it match the burn marks on your wall from the time your toaster caught fire when you tried to push an open-faced tuna melt into the slot? Will it blend in with the grime covering your window screens, so the next tenant no longer knows where the wall ends and the outside world begins?

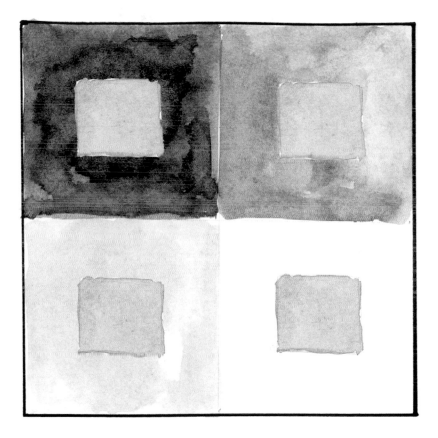

"Figures. I find a secret room in my apartment,
but it's also filled with junk."

Will Your Stuff Fit into Your New Apartment?

Congratulations! You defied all the odds and landed yourself a New York City apartment. And it even has a window! But now you have the daunting task of paring down decades-worth of Old Navy hoodies and mismatched dishes to move into a space the size of a shipping crate.

1. Where do you store your clothes?

A) Each designer item is hand-wrapped in tissue and stored in temperature-controlled containers

B) In a dresser you got from your grandmother's dead friend Ida's estate sale

C) In a knapsack under your pillow

2. How many pairs of shoes do you own?

A) Depends – are we talking Fall 2021 or Spring 2022 collections?

B) About ten, even though you wear the same pair of ballet flats every day

C) A pair of sneakers and flip-flops, but the sneakers are mostly "for show"

3. What do your bookshelves look like?

A) The library in *Beauty and the Beast*

B) A few rows of chick-lit and Agatha Christie tucked behind your ex's copy of *Infinite Jest*

C) All your books are stored neatly on the shelves – in your memory (and on your e-reader)

4. What cookware can you NOT live without?

A) Your 46-piece iron skillet set, your 10-gallon soup tureen, your pizza oven, and your antique spatula collection

B) The 1970s Corningware set you got from Ida's estate sale

C) Your GrubHub app

5. What is your bed like?

A) A California king with a headboard and foot ottoman

B) A self-lofted, full-sized bed on the box spring that came on the store's floor model

C) A sleeping bag stuffed in an old pillowcase

6. How many photos do you display?

A) Individual pics of you with every friend and family member on one of those giant collage frames

B) A group shot from your college reunion, and one with your ex (Did you break up? It's confusing.)

C) *Ha ha*, please. Do you look like a hoarder?

7. What is the biggest piece of furniture you own?

A) Your 9-piece sectional couch that wraps around your 85-inch flat-screen with surround sound

B) The upright piano you took from Ida's sitting room

C) Your microwave/cupboard/clothes steamer

8. What do you currently use your bathtub for?

A) *Um*, taking long, luxurious bubble baths

B) Storing the shoes you don't wear regularly

C) A guest bedroom

9. What's really in that cardboard box you lug around with you from apartment to apartment?

A) Every cord and charger for every computer and phone you've ever owned

B) A few old anniversary cards from your ex, and a photo of your childhood dog, Snickers

C) Whatever was in that suitcase in *Pulp Fiction*

10. Describe your essential beauty products.

A) Like, if the entirety of Sephora vomited onto a vanity

B) Your 2-in-1 dandruff shampoo, deodorant/sunscreen, and a piña colada–flavored lip balm that is also a multivitamin

C) A pair of tweezers

Answer Key:

Mostly As: Kanye West called. He wants his delusions of grandeur back. Since you are clearly not an A-lister, hedge fund manager, or resident of Gracie Mansion, you'll need to cut your crap collection by approximately 1,000 percent.

Mostly Bs: Despite your desire to hold on to the past, you seem to have a reasonable amount of reasonably sized things. You will need to throw away all of it to fit into your new apartment.

Mostly Cs: Your aversion to material goods (and basic hygiene) will prepare you for when the only thing that can be wedged into your apartment is your actual corporeal self and nothing more.

Your Upstairs Neighbor's Daily Itinerary

"We're not sure if the upstairs neighbors are ghosts,
or just use really powerful subwoofers."

44

5:30 A.M.: Wake up to radio alarm blasting "Rock You Like a Hurricane" at full volume.

5:45 A.M.: Keep hitting snooze every few minutes, so song continuously plays in thirty-second spurts.

6:30 A.M.: Put on Doc Martens and complete ten reps of fifty jumping jacks.

7:00 A.M.: Take thirty-minute shower while singing entire score from *Wicked*, including songs written for a mezzo soprano.

7:30 A.M.: Make breakfast using every cast-iron skillet in kitchen. Drop skillets on the floor multiple times to make sure eggs and bacon are really, truly cooked.

8:00 A.M.: Watch the morning news. Make sure TV sound is at maximum setting to ensure that the whole neighborhood learns of the gorilla escape from the local zoo.

9:00 A.M.: Turn living room into a tap dance studio.

9:30 A.M.: Invite thirty lead-footed tweens into studio to practice extended tap routine to "On the Good Ship Lollipop."

10:00 A.M.: Have the tap dancers do their routine again, but add in anvil tossing for dramatic effect.

11:00 A.M.: Rearrange all the furniture to best fit feng shui practices.

11:25 A.M.: Decide the couch would bring better chi when placed on the south wall.

11:46 A.M.: Actually, it would vibe better along the northeast wall.

12:15 P.M.: For lunch, fry up a grilled cheese sandwich, but let the corners burn just long enough to set off the smoke alarm.

12:30 P.M.: Open all the windows and really take time clearing the air. Let smoke alarm run through its battery life.

1:45 P.M.: Really, the couch would spark more joy if switched with the bookcase in the sitting room.

1:55 P.M.: And was elevated on cinder blocks.

2:15 P.M.: So many cinder blocks.

3:00 P.M.: Spill a shipping crate full of marbles onto hardwood floor. Spend next hour vacuuming them all up.

4:00 P.M.: Clean apartment thoroughly by hosing down garbage cans, turning on all the taps at once, and flushing the toilet repeatedly. If water cascades through cracks in the tile and floods the apartment downstairs, blame "bad plumbing" and offer free tap-dancing lessons to make up for it.

5:00 P.M.: Feel guilty about the water incident and decide to postpone the trampolining competition. Instead, head outside and flirt with the ice-cream truck driver, so the truck (and its jingle) remains parked outside the window below for over an hour.

6:00 P.M.: Fill bathtub with hungry chihuahuas. No reason needed.

9:00 P.M.: Place subwoofers on floor in all corners of every room, so when people wonder exactly where the sound is coming from, the answer is: everywhere. Blast the bass line and turn living room into a rave. Invite the tap dancers, local Roller Derby team, and your kooky friend who has a pet mammoth.

9:45 P.M.: Teach mammoth how to tap dance.

12:00 A.M.: Close all windows and set off indoor fireworks display.

2:15 A.M.: On second thought, that couch really does belong on the east wall.

5:00 A.M.: Sneak downstairs and steal my copy of *The New York Times* left outside my door.

Where You Live

(According to the Dog You Own)

5th floor walk-up

A rent-controlled studio

Above a family-style restaurant

Next door to that building that's always under construction

Technically upstate, but can still get to the city all the time, you guys

Brooklyn

An abandoned boxcar

In the past

With your parents

47

Build-a-Roommate

Start with your best friend from college, Laura. You guys lived in a tiny dorm room together for two years, so you'll definitely be able to share a studio converted into a two-bedroom with shower curtains for doors. No problem!

This will inevitably lead to a blowup over who left coffee grinds in the sink, and who made who consistently late for a job they hate anyway? Let Laura move out to live with a different college friend who looks like a poor man's Adam Scott.

Replace with Candace, a coworker you always thought would make an excellent roomie. She owns every lamp Pottery Barn ever made (along with every movie Paul Walker ever made).

This lasts approximately six months, when you both realize that seeing someone for 24 hours a day is excruciating, you hate talking about work almost as much as you hate working, and *Joy Ride* actually has some legitimate thrills. Candace moves back to Montclair with her parents, taking every single lamp with her.

Swap her out for Ludwig, a rando you found on Craigslist, who arrived with a 50-pound cat named Banksy, a couch that didn't fit through the door and had to be abandoned in front of your building, and other people's passwords to every streaming service.

Ludwig watches a lot of TV, usually while you're at work. After asking you for an extension on the lease, you arrive home one day to find his room cleared out, all your living room furniture gone, and Banksy curled up in a corner chewing on an abandoned phone charger.

Upgrade to Kelsey, a business-school student who meets a guy on day two of orientation and essentially moves in with him. You're pretty sure she's never used that room, other than as a storage space for her clothes, and as a decoy for her religious parents.

Kelsey is the perfect roommate – she lives with you for two years, yet you've only seen her that one time when she signed the lease. Unfortunately, her business-school boyfriend eventually proposes, and she can now legitimately move in with him.

Add Tracey, your second cousin, who just got back from studying abroad in Switzerland and needs a place to crash until she finds an apartment. Her luggage hasn't arrived yet, which she deals with by washing out the same three outfits in your bathroom sink, dipping into your cosmetics, and borrowing your Burberry coat indefinitely for "work stuff."

You count down the minutes until Tracey uproots from your couch, then miss her furiously when she moves in with your great-aunt in Riverdale.

Switch Tracey out for Luke, a guy you've been seeing for six months and are pretty sure is The One. Despite the fact that you're still in the honeymoon phase of your relationship, Luke's lease in Hoboken is almost up and he's always wanted to live in the city. The fact that he's more excited about his new address than his new relationship is definitely not a red flag at all.

You and Luke break up almost immediately after he moves in, because, of course. Since he signed a twelve-month lease, he refuses to leave until it's up, so you get to watch him play video games with his college buddies on the flat-screen you bought with your work bonus. At the eleven-month mark, you meet a new guy at Sloppy Dave's Bar, change the locks, and leave a box of Luke's gaming head-sets and boxers in the hallway.

Replace Luke with . . . Banksy. You've reached a point in your life when you don't need to constantly have another person in your living space, and you can afford the rent for the studio on your own. You enjoy the liberation of answering to no one, and being able to spread out over what is essentially a space for two-fifths of a person. You're pretty sure the building doesn't allow cats, but no one's ever asked, so.

Your landlord decides to sell the building, and the new owner doubles your rent for the next year. Is anyone looking for a roommate?

"No murders today, but look—they opened a
new grocery store across the street!"

Cold Open for *Law & Order*
(Starring My Roommate and Me)

VOICE-OVER:

In the criminal justice system, the people are represented by two separate yet equally important groups: the hot police officers who investigate crimes, and the casual bystanders who stumble upon dead bodies while going about their daily lives, and are definitely not scarred emotionally by it. These are their stories.

Chung-chung!

(Two women in their early thirties, Kim and Me, sit on a legless couch propped entirely on cinder blocks, in a very small apartment. They are watching a Hallmark movie that is either The Cheerleader Murderers *or* Christmas Lovers in a Small Town. *Both are excellent options.)*

ME

Those cheerleaders are really murder-y.

KIM

Right? I hope it doesn't ruin Christmas for all the lovers they murder.

We sit and mindlessly watch the TV.

TV

Be aggressive, B-E aggressive!

Screams and stabbing sounds heard.

ME

Turning to Kim

Hey, it's your turn to take the garbage out.

KIM

It was my turn *last* month.

ME

What do you mean, *last month*? The garbage is supposed to go out every day.

KIM

That's crazy. Who has time for that?

ME

You are literally sitting on the couch, cleaning under your toenails with a MetroCard. Could you please take out the garbage?

Kim stares blankly at me.

ME

Hoisting garbage bag over shoulder

Fine. Whatever. I'll do it myself.

KIM

Wait, that's not garbage, that's the bag of stuff I've been saving for my Found Object sculpture project.

ME

Looking in bag

Broken light bulbs, empty mayonnaise jar, used tissues, banana peel . . .

KIM

Yes! That's my sculpture collection.

ME

Right. I'm throwing it away.

Head for garbage room

KIM

Jumping up off couch

Get back here with my stuff! You're just jealous because I have an artistic purpose.

Follows me to garbage room

ME

Opening dumpster

I have an artistic purpose too. It's called "Paying the Rent on Time."

KIM

If you let me finish my masterpiece, I promise I'll have the —

ME

Oh my God. Kim, shut up. Do you see that?

KIM

Looks where I'm pointing

Two rats fighting to the death over a pizza crust?

ME

Whispering

No . . . behind the dumpster . . . I think it's a body.

KIM

It's probably just a bunch of rats nesting in a pile of old clothes.

Looks closer

Nope, you're right, it's a body. What should we do?

ME

Call 9-1-1! Do you have your phone?

KIM

No. I was using it to tweet about the movie. Do you have yours?

ME

No, dammit! We should get help.

Screaming

HELP!!! DEAD BODY!!! CALL 9-1-1!!!!

A siren wails in the distance and gets louder

That was fast.

Two officers approach, Captain Olivia Benson *and* Detective Lennie Briscoe.

One is a strikingly attractive middle-aged officer, and the other is played by Mariska Hargitay.

CAPTAIN BENSON

Hi, I'm Captain Olivia Benson, and this is Detective Lennie Briscoe. Did someone call for help with a body?

KIM

Wait, isn't Detective Briscoe dead? And not even from the same show?

ME

Shut UP, Kim. Don't insult the detectives by pointing out inconsistencies in my fantasy.

To Captain Benson

Wow, you've aged really well over the years.

CAPTAIN BENSON

Thanks. Solving gruesome sex murders keeps me young.

DETECTIVE BRISCOE

Leaning over the body behind the dumpster

It looks like the victim was thirty-three-years old and was murdered while taking out her roommate's garbage.

KIM

Glaring at me

See? This is why we shouldn't take out the garbage.

CAPTAIN BENSON

Isn't thirty-three a little old to still be living with roommates?

ME

How did she die?

DETECTIVE BRISCOE

It looks like she was hit over the head with that wrench lying right next to her head.

ME

Jesus.

DETECTIVE BRISCOE

Now, we have to ask, where were you two around 11:00 p.m. last night?

KIM

Yesterday was Friday, right? At home, on the couch, binge-watching *Blue Bloods*.

DETECTIVE BRISCOE

Oh yeah? Which episode?

KIM

The one where James gets caught burgling a grocery store.

DETECTIVE BRISCOE

That's a pretty good episode.

To Benson

Her alibi checks out.

CAPTAIN BENSON

To me

Can anyone verify *your* alibi?

ME

Sheepishly

The delivery guy who brought us our six-pack of rosé.

DETECTIVE BRISCOE

Do either of you own a wrench?

ME

No! I don't own any tools at all!

KIM

I have one of those L-shaped thingies that came with my IKEA futon.

CAPTAIN BENSON

Wow, I haven't seen an Allen key since college. You should invest in more adult furniture.

KIM & ME

We will! Someday!

DETECTIVE BRISCOE

Gesturing to my garbage bag

Here. Allow me.

Tosses it into the dumpster. Glass shatters. Kim cringes.

CAPTAIN BENSON

You should probably have recycled that.

DETECTIVE BRISCOE

Pointing to the dead body

Where she's going, there's no need to save the planet.

BRISCOE & BENSON *walk away*

ME

Well, I'm going to finish watching *Christmas Murder Cheerleaders in a Small Town.*

Heads inside

KIM

Crouches down near body, but turns to the fighting rats

Are you going to eat that pizza crust?

Chung-chung!

"It doesn't really keep me warm, but it pretty
much guarantees me a seat on the train."

3

THE SHORTEST DISTANCE BETWEEN TWO POINTS IS NOT THE L TRAIN

A Guided Tour
of Youthful Mistakes

Hello, and welcome to City Gaffes, a guided tour of youthful urban folly. Feel free to hop on and off the bus whenever you want, and definitely take lots of cringe-worthy photos of my past humiliations.

Over on the left is the Medallion Corporation, where I had my first internship. Sort of! Turns out, if you don't hear from a company, it means you didn't get the job, and you probably shouldn't show up on the first day wearing your power suit from Express. *Whoops!*

Moving along . . .

Look left, and you'll see my first apartment. When I signed the lease, there was no floor in the living room, but we eventually got one. Immediately afterward, about forty mice moved into our oven. So many memories were made while shrieking and jumping on furniture that *also* housed rodents.

I lived here for six years.

And here's Metisse, a neighborhood steak joint. My roommate and I always suggested it for dates, since steak is delicious but pricey.

It mysteriously burned down a year after I moved in, remained vacant for three years, then reopened as a dialysis center.

This all happened around the time guys stopped paying for dinner.

This is the pile of garbage I vomited in after learning
that tequila and spaetzle don't mix.

(Pause for pictures.)

And over this way, to the right, is a statue in Union Square Park. Once, when I was going on a first date, the guy asked me to meet him in front of this statue. He arrived twenty minutes late, and told me he was watching me wait from the telescope in his bedroom.

We went out two more times after that.

Yeah, yeah, I *know . . . ugh.*

As I was leaving this cafe, I stumbled upon the filming of
Law & Order: SVU. I stood for two hours watching multiple takes
of Christopher Meloni chasing after a van.

Years later, I finally caught a rerun of that episode. It was super
gruesome, and I never ate at that cafe again.

This is a *different* pile of garbage I threw up in,
after chasing three rounds of Goldschläger with
a night of zydeco dancing.

This is the generic Italian restaurant in the theater district that my mom insists on going to every time she visits. I always order the chicken Francese, and it's always a disappointment.

Over here is the hole-in-the-wall jazz club where I first introduced my new boyfriend to my friends. During the bass solo, a gigantic roach scampered across our table, and without hesitation my boyfriend smashed it with my friend's glass.

Everyone agreed that he was "marriage material."

I decided to bring him home and see how he'd handle the silverfish situation in my bathtub.

This is the post where I chained up my bike.
At least I think it is. Maybe it's the next block?

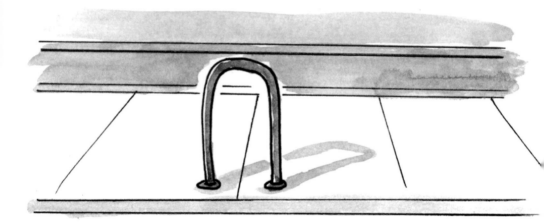

Over to the right . . .

I was buying a six-dollar latte when I noticed I was in line behind Christopher Meloni. I racked my brain for something to say. Finally, as he was leaving, I stepped in front of him and mumbled, "Thanks for saving that lady in the van." Then I ran out of the coffee shop.

At least I'm pretty sure it was Christopher Meloni. . . .

Over here is the first subway I ever rode on. Please note that this is heading uptown and not downtown (where I was supposed to go).

Wait, I see a lot of you are exiting the tour now. Did you just hop on the bus so it would take you to the subway? *Well-played, tourists.*

Thank you for joining us at City Gaffes!* Tours leave
continuously on the hour, so you can witness me
making the same mistakes over, and over, and over. . . .

*Tip your driver!

Oddly Specific New York City Neighborhoods

Service Changes on Every Train Line This Weekend

Until early 2035, the 1 train will be skipping all stops along Broadway, except on weekends, when it will make ONLY stops on Broadway, and skip all other stops.

D trains will run local in both directions, sometimes adding stops that aren't even on the map!

Service on the R and N trains will be suspended overnight throughout the summer months, since it's really, really hot on the platforms.

3 trains will be experiencing delayed service for the next two weeks in observance of George Pullman's birthday, the inventor of the steam engine.

Due to platform construction, the 7 train will be skipping Roosevelt Avenue, where all the transfers to Manhattan-bound trains are. To get to Manhattan, Segways will be provided just outside the subway entrance. Segway rentals will be an additional sixteen-dollars each way.

2 trains will skip all Brooklyn-bound stops this winter. Take a shuttle or Segway to the bus terminal on Flatbush Avenue, and transfer to one of nine buses that will take you within eleven blocks of your destination.

G trains now essentially function as M trains, but passengers still won't want to ride it anywhere.

Hitch a ride to **Rockaway Beach**, the bus ride is too slow.

This weekend, 4 trains are 5 trains, **5** trains are 6 trains, and 6 trains are relics of a distant, but more robust transportation system.

L trains will continue to make sporadic appearances if and when they choose, despite there being nothing inherently wrong with them.

Q train lines have been extended up to Ninety-Sixth Street, for the nine people who still ride the Q train.

Penn Station has a new sandwich shop that's worth checking out.

C and E trains are running just fine, thank you, but remember: The cars are empty *for a reason*.

From 12:01 a.m. to 5:00 a.m. Saturday, Sunday, and Monday, for all of April and May, shuttle buses will replace 3 trains between Times Square and Harlem due to track work. As an alternative, never leave your apartment.

Brooklyn Road Test

1. **To check your blind spots, you should consult:**

   A) The empty space where your side mirror used to be

   B) Your childhood best friend Bryce, who's sitting in the back seat

   C) Estella, your psychic

2. **The following alcoholic beverages will give you a blood alcohol content of more than .08, the legal limit:**

   A) Seventeen bottles of craft beer from the microbrewery set up in the old glass factory

   B) Two glasses of pinot grigio you bought on a bachelorette trip to the North Fork

   C) The cider you fermented from the homegrown pears in your window box

3. **The following vehicles may drive in a bike lane (check all that apply):**

   A) Citi Bikes

   B) Lyft

   C) Penny-farthings

   D) Razor scooters

   E) Powder-blue Vespa with child's seat in back

   F) Personal drones

   G) Honda Civics

4. On multiple-laned roads, the far-right lane is used for:

A) Uber Eats deliverymen

B) Passing the slow-driving tourists trying to locate the botanical gardens

C) Sidestepping the U-Haul truck moving a rolltop desk into that brownstone you had your eye on

5. Your wheels should be pointed straight ahead unless you are:

A) Swerving to avoid a Steinway that's found its way onto the street

B) Jamming to Arcade Fire

C) Navigating Barclays Center traffic

6. If your car begins to skid, you should:

A) Close your eyes and mentally refresh your meditation app

B) Make a mental note to leave your vinyl collection to your ex

C) Turn into the skid, then keep turning that way. *Wheeee!*

7. You should honk at another car when:

A) They've been sitting at an intersection for ten minutes waiting for another car to flash their lights at them

B) Your child ALSO is a public school Gifted & Talented student

C) They come to a complete stop to allow the guy walking four labradoodles to cross

8. When there are double solid lines next to your lane, you are allowed to:

A) Change lanes if no one's looking and you're slick about it

B) Make an illegal nine-point turn because you drove right past that unmarked sake shop

C) Double-park next to that fire truck that is *also* double-parked

9. If your tire goes flat while driving, you must:

A) Pull up in front of a bar and have a few bespoke single-hopped IPAs while waiting for your mom's AAA road-side assistance

B) Keep driving. Now both your front tires match!

C) Pull to the side. It's hard to ride a unicycle without air.

Look Up, Look Down

Look up, there's the instantly recognizable sign for the iconic restaurant where you're meeting your friend for dinner.

Look down, there's an automatic door sensor in the exact spot you've been standing, and the hostess is starting to get pissed.

Look up, there's a traffic light you've never noticed on this street you've crossed at least 100 times.

Look down, there's a crosswalk you've never used on this street you've crossed at least 100 times.

Look up, there's a countdown clock for something that might be End of Days, but is probably an esoteric art instillation.

Look down, the heel of your knockoff Louboutins is caught in a sewer grate.

Look up, it's definitely that kid from *Stranger Things*, or someone who looks just like him.

Look down, check your phone to see if your facial recognition app can confirm it's him.

Look up, there's a flock of incontinent pigeons congregating on the bodega awning exactly above your head.

Look down, there's a fleet of rodents dashing between the building dumpster and the garbage bags on the curb.

Look up, there's an elderly man wearing the exact sweater you just purchased from H&M.

Look down, maybe he won't notice that you're both twinning it up today. Nope, he notices.

Look up, the rain that splattered your coat is just the runoff from other people's air conditioners.

Look down, the dark, sooty polka dots on the concrete are definitely a historical tour of other people's gum.

Look up, you feel a sense of warmth and comfort arriving at your apartment building.

Look down, try not to trip over the people hanging out on your stoop, none of whom actually live in your building.

Look up, the glow of the lights from the buildings speckling the bridges and glittering on the water make you thrilled to be a part of something so vibrant, so magical, so utterly *alive*.

Look down, how many blocks did you walk with a used condom stuck to the underside of your boot?

Let Me Tell You about Queens

"Where in Queens do you live?"

"Oh, my grandparents live there, in a co-op not too far from you."

"You should check out the Unisphere in Flushing Meadows–Corona Park. It's from the 1964 World's Fair."

"I'm not sure exactly what the World's Fair was. I think other countries came, and there were rides, like 'It's a Small World'?"

"No, I don't think the Unisphere was a ride."

"My grandmother was at one of the World's Fairs, I can ask her next time I see her."

"No, don't park there — it's a Tuesday."

"You have to try the Thai restaurants in Jackson Heights, they're more authentic than actual Thailand. But don't order anything with more than three red peppers next to it; you don't have the practice."

"Jackson Diner isn't really a diner."

"PS 1 isn't really an elementary school."

"Don't park there either; it's Monday between 4:30 and 6:30 p.m."

"Julie's grandparents live here, too! They've lived in their building for forty-seven years."

"I told you, it's illegal to park next to a cemetery."

"Shake Shack in Citi Field is worth sitting through a Mets game for."

"You should have Greek food on Ditmars Boulevard in Astoria. No, there's definitely no parking there."

"The Tudor homes are really nice in Forest Hills Gardens. They filmed those scenes in *The Marvelous Mrs. Maisel* where her parents slummed it in Queens and complained about what a dump it was, right in that medieval-looking mansion with the turrets!"

"There are multiple stops near Jamaica Center on three different train lines that will take you to two separate places."

"Jonathan's grandparents lived around here, too, before they died. They're buried in that cemetery your car was towed from."

"There are no universities in College Point."

"Have you ever seen the U.S. Open? It's pretty cool, although it was crowded and hard to see, and I don't really know tennis well and had no idea who the players were. But you have to see a game sometime!"

"*Match.* I meant, you have to see a match sometime. Sorry. Whatever."

"Everything nice in Queens probably originated as an attraction at the World's Fair."

"Katie's grandparents live on Seventy-First Street, not Seventy-First Avenue. And clearly not Seventy-First Road."

"It will take you three traffic light cycles to cross Queens Boulevard, so you're better off finding something to do on your side of the street."

"It's probably *not* a great idea to hitch a ride to Rockaway Beach."

"I'm looking for an outfit that says I'm serious about my job until absolutely anything else comes along."

4

ALL WORK AND NO PLAY MAKES JANE STILL UNABLE TO PAY HER RENT

Things You Wish You Could List as "Special Skills" on Your Resume

Beating an extra-hard level in Candy Crush without the use of boosters.

The ability to eat sushi using only chopsticks, even when a loosely packed roll dissolves in the soy sauce.

Recognizing a *Law & Order* rerun less than five minutes into the episode, and sometimes even recalling the verdict.

Being able to identify what gum people are chewing, based on the way their breath smells. Except for Chiclets, which, after thirty seconds, become tasteless, odorless tar blocks.

Still remembering the phone numbers of your childhood best friend, the cute lifeguard from Camp Tallahassee, and your childhood pizza place that has since been turned into a tutoring center.

À la *The Breakfast Club*, applying your ChapStick to the underside of your chin by balancing it in your cleavage and moving your face back and forth.

Drinking three Appletinis without getting the hiccups.

Being able to rattle off the current CVs of each cast member of *Game of Thrones*.

Guessing the date of the leftovers in your fridge based on its position on the shelf and strength of odor.

Correctly picking the movie that will win the Academy Award every single year, for the past two years.

Doing a spot-on impression of Mr. Potter from *It's a Wonderful Life*, no matter what anyone else tells you.

Being able to predict your next menstrual cycle with a margin of error of plus or minus one week.

Unlocking your apartment door using only an expired MetroCard.

Knowing the jingle from every popular commercial that aired between 1996 and 2007.

Choosing the longest checkout line at the grocery store.

All the Buttons on Your Work Phone

(and What They Do)

1. **Hold indefinitely.**

2. **Hold indefinitely**, while Hall & Oates's "Private Eyes" plays.

3. **Speaker volume**, to be used if you've shoved a turkey sandwich in your mouth just as a client calls.

4. **Transfer** calls to your coworker Mike's phone, since he's been playing *Assassin's Creed* behind his spreadsheet for the past hour and a half.

5. **Change "Hold" music** to a more on-the-nose Hall & Oates song, like "Out of Touch."

6. **Mute**, so no one hears you practice the lyrics to "Guns and Ships" from *Hamilton* during a conference call.

7. **Speed-dial**, for your team manager, work husband Eric, and the only Au Bon Pain that delivers.

8. **Conference call**, for setting up multiple simultaneous conversations that you will inevitably get confused by, and wind up shit talking Caroline while she's on the line.

9. **Redial**, to call back your therapist to ask if you could split your forty-five-minute session into three fifteen-minute sessions, squeezed in between client meetings.

10. **Intercom**, so your officemates can hear that the HR rep calling you about your paycheck kind of sounds like Christopher Walken.

11. **Do Not Disturb**, to turn off your phone while you're talking to Dr. Longman on your cell. It's not that you have trust issues; it's just that you already told everyone about your weird Harry Potter dream over lunch and don't want to bore them with the details, *again*.

12. **Play back your voice messages** to see if 1993 called and wants its technology back.

Notes From Your Morning Meeting

Whoa, why is my head so much bigger than everyone else's?

OK, my head size is better. Now, how do I center myself?

Well, this is a better angle ... Aah! My head's too big again!

There's a toothpaste stain on my shirt. Now I have to position myself so it's off-camera.

Keep facing forward so they can't tell I'm checking my phone.

I wonder where Laura got her couch.

Oh man, this meeting
is boring.
Must... look... alert...

Cover mouth with hand so
no one sees me yawn.

Maybe I'll turn off my
video and grab coffee.

Much better.

Ooh, is that Jonah? In a hoodie? Not too shabby, Jonah.

Hm. It's a Princeton hoodie. Well-played, Jonah.

Why is everyone smiling?
Should I smile?
Not too wide.
Ha ha ha. Fun!
My head's too big again.
Pull back... center... tilt...
PERFECT.

I bet Laura's couch isn't covered in marinara stains and Bloody Mary mix.

Well, guess I better unmute myself and say something.

Dammit.

How to Sleep-Train the City

New York City is the city that doesn't sleep. And by now, you and everyone else is pretty damn tired. Delirious with sleep-deprivation, frustration, and the sound of four drunk bankers fighting over an Uber, it's time to buckle down and put this urban playground to bed.

When Should You Start Sleep-Training?

Now. Aren't you tired?

I mean, it's best to establish proper sleep routines right away. But judging from the fact you're currently sprawled on your ex-boyfriend's futon until you "find something afford-able," old habits are hard to break with, especially when they look like Shawn Mendes.

Is Sleep-Training the City Safe?

Both you and the City are trapped in a toxic relationship that leads to mutual exhaustion and resentment. Attempting to run down the subway steps and fling yourself onto a packed uptown D train on only two hours' of sleep is waaaay more dangerous than sleep-training.

Besides, everyone knows that nothing good happens in the city after 2:00 a.m. Sleep-training makes everything safer.

What Are Some Common Sleep-Training Methods?

The goal of sleep-training is to get the City to fall asleep on its own, and stay asleep. While this is no easy feat (especially with all the after-hours clubs in the Meatpacking District), there are some tried-and-true techniques that have proven effective.

A. Cry It Out

Picture it: It's Sunday night, and you're heading home after meeting friends for dinner, but you notice there's a new indie bookstore that opened up near your apartment. After reading the endings of three books without purchasing them, you continue on your way and discover a new cookie shop that offers at least three peanut butter flavors. After stuffing your face with the brick-sized delectables, you pass by your favorite haunt. You swear you're only popping in for one drink, but the Pixies are on the jukebox, and the next thing you know it's 4:00 a.m. and your alarm is going to go off in an hour. It's enough to make anyone cry.

Which is exactly what you should do.

Scream at the top of your lungs until the bookstore shutters its door in horror. Cry until your eye ducts flush out the crumbs from the Insomnia Cookies. Bawl until no one can hear the faint strumming of "Here Comes Your Man" over your bone-weary wails. You'll see significant improvement after a week. Before you know it, the City will exhaust itself of your yelling and turn off the lights at a normal hour (except for Times Square, which has no off position, and is already accustomed to the sound of tears).

B. The Ferber Method

This sleep-training technique involves letting the City go to sleep a few minutes earlier each day. On Night #1, go to the all-night theater to see a midnight showing of *Blade Runner: Director's Cut*. On Night #2, go see a normal movie at a normal hour, like that new Liam Neeson action flick where he saves someone. On Night #3, check out the first matinee for that Nancy Meyers movie.

Pretty soon, your movie-watching will be wrapped up before lunchtime. You'll still see movies, but you'll have no desire to sit through the self-indulgent butchering of otherwise cool films. Pretty soon, the theater will stop their "Midnite Feature," directors will stop remastering their masterpieces, and everyone will be in bed by 9:00 p.m.

C. Establish a Routine and Stick to It

Consistency is key. If you've sworn off ordering midnight hoagies from the corner bodega, you need to stick with that. Even slipping up once, after coming home sloshed from a work event and craving garlic knots, can throw off the new routine and set the City back to its old habits.

D. Don't Respond to Every Little Noise or Sound

For years, you've woken up multiple times a night to deal with city sounds: an unexpected buzz on your apartment intercom, a cop car with its lights illuminating your bedroom like a criminal discotheque, the ice-cream truck parked right outside your window, still inexplicably drawing in the awake children. All this cacophonous nonsense leaves you wide awake, and also craving a Chipwich at 3:00 a.m.

Get some noise-canceling headphones and block it out. The FOMO is real, but you're not missing out on anything important. Your upstairs neighbor Craig forgot his key again and needs you to buzz him in. The cops aren't even arresting anyone—they're just chatting with the bodega owner about what kind of cat he has. And that ice-cream truck needs to move it along—no child should be eating sugar at 11:00 p.m. on a school night.

Sleep training will be a difficult transition for both you and the City. But with consistency, trickery, and luck, the City will soon be sleeping peacefully, and you will have learned the valuable life skill of how to sleep in a place that sounds like an apocalyptic construction site every single night.

"I think we can both agree this was a huge mistake."

5

FINDING LOVE IN A HOPELESS PLACE

Dating Urban Legends

I.   A woman says goodnight to her date and hops into her Uber. As they creep along Third Avenue, a pair of high beams from the cab behind her illuminate the car. She stops updating her Insta with pictures of her entrée and stares behind her, but the beams turn off.

The Uber makes a right down Seventy-Sixth Street, and the cab follows. Suddenly, the back seat is once again flooded with light. The woman whips around, but the beams turn off just as suddenly. The woman is now apprehensive, and for the rest of the ride, sits tensely as the high beams turn on and off.

When the Uber pulls up in front of her apartment, she asks the driver to stick around for a minute, then jumps out and stalks over to the cab. Her date from earlier in the evening gets out and says he just wanted to make sure she got home safe. The woman tells him she's touched by his thoughtfulness, but is secretly horrified, and runs inside. She then deletes his contact info from her phone and never sees him again.

II.   Before a big date, a girl locks her bathroom door and turns off the lights. She stands in front of the mirror and spins around three times, chanting "Bloody Mary, Bloody Mary, Bloody Mary." She then looks in the mirror, but instead of conjuring the spirit of Bloody Mary, Portender of Futures, it's just her roommate Laurel, who was trying to tweeze her upper lip when the girl barged in.

III. A Brooklyn woman spends the night with her new boyfriend. As she settles under his Star Wars duvet, she hears a faint scraping sound coming from under the bed. She immediately panics, thinking it's the Red Hook Man, a serial killer who hides under couples' beds in rent-stabilized apartments and waits for them to fall asleep before murdering them with his hook hand, thus releasing the apartments back on the market.

Scrape . . . scrape . . . scrape . . .

She leaps out of bed, tripping over a Nintendo Switch and Razor scooter, and shines her cell phone flashlight under the bed to catch the Red Hook Man in the act. But it turns out the scraping noise was from a pair of mice screwing inside a bike helmet.

IV. A girl works as an au pair for twin boys in Morningside Heights. One day, while trying to figure out how to turn on their fancy TV, she receives a mysterious text telling her how beautiful she is. Not knowing the identity of the sender, the girl doesn't write back.

The next day, while the twins meet with their Latin tutor, she gets another text from the same number, complimenting her melodic voice. Creeped out, but also weirdly flattered, the girl types back "TY" with a Winky-face emoji. The unknown texter replies with a Devilish Grin emoji, and they spend the rest of the morning volleying flirty texts back and forth.

After a few days of chatting, the girl suggests meeting "IRL," and the phantom texts abruptly stop. Hurt, the girl has her friend who worked at the Genius Bar at the Apple Store trace the number, and it turns out

. . . the texts were coming from inside the house.

The twin boys lose all phone privileges for a week, and the girl quits her job as an au pair and goes back to school for speech pathology.

V. A group of women out for the night are joined by a handsome, ghostlike man who uses them to get past the bouncer of the club. Once inside, the women look around for him, trying to get him to buy the first round, but realize he's disappeared.

The next week, the same group of women is heading out to dinner when the man materializes again. He recommends a trendy and expensive neo-fusion restaurant, and then proceeds to order shared plates for the table. When it comes time to split the check, suddenly, the man just . . . vanishes.

Later that night, a young lady meets up with the gorgeous apparition she matched with on KindredSpirits. After a night of cocktails and dancing, she brings him back to her place. The next morning, when she goes to make coffee, she notices that the man is gone. She checks her dating app, and his profile is also gone. When she contacts customer service, she's informed that no such account ever existed. As she sips her coffee and refreshes her browser, her fingers graze a phantom hickey on her neck, and she wonders if it was all a dream.

VI. While scrolling through her social media posts, a woman notices a tall, spectral being in a suit and tie, with a white, featureless face, lurking in the shadows of all her pictures. They start dating and become engaged in less than a year. They now live in a four-bedroom Tudor in Westchester and are expecting their first child.

VII. Two close friends turn forty and are still single, so they marry each other. One of them is a chupacabra.

"Look, I just don't think we're compatible. I'm a carnivorous predator, and you're a Sagittarius."

Metropolitan Meet-Cutes

Whoops, wrong meeting! But before I go, let me add that I, too, loved *Where the Crawdads Sing.*

Ways to Describe Yourself in a Dating App

(without Using a Photo)

My eyes are the color of the Hudson River, especially the part in upstate New York where they dump the nuclear runoff.

I have the pale yet flushed complexion of a practicing autoerotic asphyxiator.

I'm flaxen-haired, like the character from *The Princess Bride*. No, not Princess Buttercup, but the raspy dude who tortures Westley.

I have the high-wattage smile of Julia Roberts's spider character from *Charlotte's Web*.

My body is both enveloping and hard, like a Tempur-Pedic pillow stuffed with billiard balls.

My legs go on forever, which makes them really annoying to get stuck in a conversation with at dinner parties.

My ex would describe me as a 10, referring to where he'd rank me among the candidates for mayor of NYC.

I have the physique of a snake in the process of digesting a water buffalo.

I'm young at heart, I but have the bone density of a much older woman.

My body is less the traditional hourglass figure, and more of an egg timer, set to go off once the spinach frittata is ready to come out of the oven.

My friends would describe me as someone who's "up for anything, as long as it involves watching *Blue Bloods* reruns."

I have limbs made for dancing to the beat of my own drummer, whose name is Raul, plays in a German hard-core punk band, and lives in the apartment right above mine.

I routinely consume salads that contain at least four different kinds of lettuce. I've also invented a sandwich made from Nutella, marshmallow fluff, and the center of a Cadbury Creme Egg.

My celebrity doppelganger is the female hood ornament duetting with the Allstate insurance driver on Pet Shop Boys's "Opportunities."

I have an ass that doesn't quit; it prefers to get fired, so it can then collect unemployment.

I'm a tall drink of vodka tonic in a sea of short whiskey sours.

"He's not my type, but in a classic rom-com sort of way."

Future Rom-Coms Set in NYC

How to Find a Guy in 10 Years

Columnist Abbie Abernathy is looking to move up at the magazine she works for, writing more fulfilling and hard-hitting pieces. Her editor finally assigns her big break: track down runaway Wall Street scion Bart Bartholomew and bring him back to his shipping magnate parents. But while finding love is easy, finding a crooked banker who skipped bail on an embezzlement charge and has at least six passports, is hard.

Will Abbie get her man? And if so, how long will it take?

When Harry Met Sally's Therapist

After college graduation, Harry and Sally meet and spend eighteen hours together in a Zipcar headed to New York. They don't get along, particularly after Harry goes on and on about how a man and a woman can never be just friends because he'll always want to have sex with her. Sally isn't sure what to make of Harry, especially when she bumps into him on a flight a few years later, and he's still yammering on about male/female dynamics and wanting to pork all his gal pals. Sick of his TMI and relationship mansplaining, Sally introduces Harry to her therapist, Dr. Longman, who starts Harry on twice-a-week psychotherapy and 10 mL of Lexapro. When they bump into each other a few years later, Harry is in a happier, healthier place, and they enjoy spending platonic time together at famous NYC landmarks.

You've Got DMs

Indie blogger Kelly Katherine hates Jerry Faber, CEO of *Spade*, a huge online magazine trying to buy her out. When she swipes right on a hot writer on slandr, she ignites an intense, steamy no-strings-attached affair that knocks her back on her heels. Will Kelly discover the identity of her sexy writer? Will Jerry realize he misses being on the other side of the byline? Will carpal tunnel and repetitive stress syndrome get in the way of their physical connection?

Two Years' Notice

Urban planning specialist Wade Gregg partners up with billionaire Kelsey Luck to turn an abandoned mental hospital into an orphanage and community garden. When working for a powerful female begins to trouble Wade, he gives notice while trying to find another job working in his field. Two years later, the paperwork for the orphanage still hasn't gone through, and Wade has exhausted every lead, contact, and LinkedIn connection he has. As he nears forty and struggles to put together some semblance of a career path, he has second thoughts about leaving Kelsey, his health benefits, and 401(k).

13 Going on 40

Teenager Jenny Lucas dreams of bypassing the horrors of middle school straight into adulthood, which she knows will be "amazingly perfect!" After making a wish in a fountain, she wakes up with a horrible pain in her lower back. Jen finds herself slogging through a stressful forty-five-minute subway commute, mind-numbing meetings at a midlevel job she hates, back-to-back parent-teacher conferences for her surly tween kids, and the joys of cooking hot dogs in a pot of water. Will forty be the "flirty, fun-filled fantasy" she dreamed of? Or will Jenny regret bypassing college and her twenties and jumping right into the mortgage-filled soul-suck of middle age?

Splash

A young boy is terrified by a giant bug he found clinging to his shower curtain. Years later, the roach, now the size of a human, seeks him out, and they fall in love. Will he choose his life as an ad exec, with his partner and kids, or life in a sewage drain with his Kafkaesque true love?

Moonstruck

Widow Lorraine accepts a marriage proposal from her boy-friend Jasper, but finds herself falling for his younger brother Remi. After sharing a night of passion, she feels guilty, but none of this matters because the full moon causes all three of them, along with Lorraine's Italian American family, to turn into werewolves. When Remi loses a hand to a silver bullet fired by Jasper, Lorraine finds herself losing her heart.

Planning Your NYC Wedding

"I get it. You're engaged."

Submit an engagement photo to *The New York Times* Sunday Styles section. Make sure you mention all the Ivy League colleges you applied to, give yourself middle names even though neither of you have one, and share your romantic tale of how you met-cute while you were riding an up escalator at Macy's and he passed you on the down-escalator.

Choose a place for your reception. There are lots of classic restaurants and party venues to choose from, but how romantic would it be to get married under the stars at Grand Central Terminal? Guests will be transported from The Plaza Hotel to the reception via Gordon Gekko's limo from *Wall Street*.

Dress your bridesmaids in traditional NYC colors (muted gray with LED lights in the bodice), and drag your gal-pal entourage to Kleinfeld Bridal so they can witness you saying "YES!" to the dress, and "SWEET BABY JESUS" to the price tag.

Next, focus on the design of your big day. Pick flowers from the Brooklyn Botanical Garden for the bouquets and tie them together with Tiffany's tennis bracelets. For centerpieces, place Statue of Liberty snow globes in the center of each table, and sprinkle cherry blossoms from the Hudson River Greenway around them. Fashion tablecloths out of the thick velvet curtains from Radio City Music Hall. Cover up the train timetables with giant billboards advertising all your favorite couple things: Pepsi, the musical *Newsies*, *Double Shot at Love*, and Nasdaq. Choose a favor that epitomizes your city flavor: McSorley's glasses filled with Bubba Gump shrimp.

The food will be an eclectic blend of traditional New York City fare: mini hot dogs from a cart, pretzels, Lombardi's pizza, Peter Luger steaks, and fresh fish farmed from the East River. The bar will only serve Manhattans, and the wedding cake will have three tiers – the first made of raw gourmet cookie dough, the second a cheesecake from Junior's, and the top layer a cronut.

Choose "New York State of Mind" for your first dance. Spend the night gettin' down with your nearest and dearest to every single Frank Sinatra song ever made, including B sides and covers.

Weddings are all about showcasing who you really are: a city girl to the core. And while your fiancé may have shot down your other wedding theme ideas of "Bermuda Triangle" and "CSI: Wedding Reception," this is your chance to let the world know that you live in the city! And the city lives in you.

6

THE QUINTESSENTIAL NEW YORK THANKSGIVING DAY PARADE

Hi, I'm Savannah, and this is Al, and welcome to the quintessential New York Thanksgiving Day Parade! This year, the floats and balloons are sponsored by the city itself, to represent characters that are indelibly etched in our collective urban memories.

Al: First up, we have the Blue Whale, made famous by taking up an entire floor of the American Museum of Natural History.

Savannah: Yes, Al, tourists travel from all over the world to get a glimpse of the biggest animal ever to exist. At more than 21,000 pounds, this sea creature has been delighting and towering over people since the 1960s.

Al: And coming up behind the Blue Whale, we have the infamous Pizza Rat! Gaining notoriety for dragging a slice of pizza down some subway stairs, the Pizza Rat exploded on social media and became quite the star.

Savannah: That's right, Al. This little guy was viewed more than 5 million times.

Al: Didn't you dress up as a sexy Pizza Rat for Halloween that year?

Savannah: No comment, Al.

Al: Wave hello to the Lemon Ice King of Corona and his queen! What a beautiful family, what a beautiful business.

Savannah: Look, they're spraying the crowd with strawberry ices. That probably seemed like a good idea before they started.

Al: It's starting to look like a crime scene here.

Savannah: A delicious, sticky crime scene. Making children happy for decades.

Al: Ooh, here comes Pale Male, the red-tailed hawk that lives nestled in a building on Fifth Avenue across the street from Central Park.

Savannah: Pizza Rat better watch out for this huge apex predator, who clearly found rent-stabilized digs.

Al: Clearly. Now make way, coming up is a fiberglass cow, one of many that were decorated and placed around New York City more than two decades ago in the Cow Parade.

Savannah: And they're back. This one looks like it was decorated by Yayoi Kusama.

Al: What a weird tradition.

Savannah: And now comes Scabby the Rat, a popular inflatable that's present at all buildings with major labor disputes.

Al: Get a load of his beady red eyes and fierce determination. Wouldn't want to cross *that* picket line. What's next, Savannah?

Savannah: I do believe we have a Leo *and* a Gemini in the house!

Al: I don't know what you mean.

Savannah: The lions from the New York Public Library. Patience and Fortitude are making their way down Fifth Avenue.

Al: I still don't get your reference.

Savannah: Whatever. Oh look, representing the borough of Staten Island, it's *Saturday Night Live*'s very own character, Pete Davidson.

Al: He's still on that show?

Savannah: I have no idea. I guess it's the best Staten Island has to offer? Looming at a lanky 6 feet 3 inches, he's gracing the parade with a dazed joviality that barely masks a deep-seated anger.

Al: Now *that* is quintessential New York.

Savannah: It sure is, Al. And finally, closing out this year's parade, is a staple of New York City, all dressed in red, shaking his belly like a bowl full of jelly.

Al: Santa?

Savannah: Guess again! He's a permanent fixture in the Times Square photography circuit. Look, he's posing with some tourists right now!

Al: Thank you so much for joining us this year for the quintessential New York Thanksgiving Day Parade. Stay tuned for *The NYC Dog Show*, featuring Roscoe the Bed Bug–Sniffing Dog, and the drug-detecting dogs at JFK.

"Someone needs to tell Claudia this doesn't
count as 'meeting for brunch.'"

URBAN SPRAWLIN'

City Dining
Math Problems

1. **For her birthday**, Caitlin made a reservation at a tapas place for six people at 8:00 p.m. If five people show up at 8:00 p.m., and one person shows up at 9:45 p.m., what time will the party be seated?

2. **There are six chairs** at the table. Caitlin sits in the middle since it's *her day*. If Jane and Dori want to sit on either side of Asher, Kyle wants to sit across from Dori so they can share the tempeh dish that Eater recommended, and Luke wants to sit near a window so he can surreptitiously smoke the Cuban he stole from work, whose thigh does Caitlin "accidentally" graze when she reaches for her purse?

3. **Each pitcher of sangria** pours approximately six glasses. If Jane gave up alcohol for her month-long cleanse, Luke is pounding them back, Caitlin is mixing the red and white to make "birthday rose-gria," and Dori only wants to eat the brandy-soaked pears from the top, how many pitchers should they order?

4. **The orange-and-lavender-glazed meatball tapa** comes with three meatballs. If Dori is vegan this week, Luke is a gluttonous monster, and Caitlin deserves a whole one since today's her *you know what*, how many microscopic pieces will the remaining two meatballs be divided into?

5. **Luke is telling the story** about the time he almost got arrested for urinating in a firehouse. All members of the party except Jane have heard this story before, although not all at the same time. How many times has Luke told his story?

6. **As a main course**, all six friends split one goat cheese and sun-dried tomato flatbread (although Dori picks off the goat cheese). How many blocks will they walk after dinner to find an open pizza place?

7. **There is only one stall** in the women's bathroom. There are nine women in front of Jane in line. How long will she wait before sneaking into the unoccupied men's room?

    **Bonus: How many women in line also went to Jane's small liberal-arts college even though they didn't know each other there? Small world, right?

8. **When the waiter keeps passing by** holding plates of whipped-cream dollops with candles in them, how many times will Caitlin think it's for her?

9. **The bill comes to $545.18,** and Asher wants to put the whole thing on his credit card. Luke left early and only threw $20 on the table despite consuming one whole pitcher of sangria by himself. The birthday girl shouldn't have to pay, and Dori refuses to split the bill evenly since she didn't have any meatballs, sangria, or goat cheese. Kyle can't convince the bartender to break a $100 bill, and Jane wants to Venmo her share of the check to Asher. How much will Asher end up paying for dinner, yet again?

10. **After dinner,** the remaining friends debate where to go next. Kyle has to work early tomorrow but will "totally hang for one more drink" if someone has change for $100. Caitlin hopes someone will buy her a "birthday-tini" at a swanky new lounge. Asher suggests a dive bar named Sloppy Dave's, and Jane and Dori prefer to go with him since he looks like a slightly beat Paul Rudd (and Caitlin's birthday mercifully ended at midnight). How long will they stand in an indecisive circle in front of the restaurant?

11. **The next day,** which will get more "likes":

    Caitlin's post "Thx 4 all the birthday love! #HumbleAndLucky," or a picture of the meatball dish on Jane's Instagram?

"There are literally no celebrities left that
I want to cheat on my boyfriend with."

Celebrity Spottings Around Town

Turns out the distinguished gentleman you've been eyeing across Le Pain Quotidien isn't Antonio Banderas, but your AP Spanish teacher, who you haven't seen in more than fifteen years. He recognizes you immediately, and you have a forced conversation in stilted Spanish where you opt not to conjugate any verbs and exit by saying you need to *ir a la playa*.

The girl at the table next to you at Haru is definitely Anna Kendrick, and when you try to snap a selfie and somehow get her in the background, you find she's hiding behind the sashimi menu.

You're pretty sure the woman behind you in the pharmacy line at CVS is the woman from the insurance commercial who thinks her husband is having an affair with "Jake from State Farm." You're also pretty sure that, based on her prescription, she has a UTI.

After extensive googling, you learn the man sitting a row behind you at the latest Star Wars movie is in fact actor John C. Reilly, who, despite having more than 200 acting credits, has not appeared in anything you've actually seen.

After enlarging the surreptitious pic you took on your phone, you discover the person crossing Houston in the far distance is just some random old woman, and *not*, as you told all your friends, Sir Paul McCartney.

Everyone working at the Sbarros near Madison Square Garden has been a guest actor on *Law & Order: SVU*. The delivery guy has been a perp in at least two episodes, so you cut him a wide berth as he carries the pies outside.

The man washing his hands in the theater bathroom is definitely Mark Ruffalo, because it looks like him, and also because you followed him into the men's room after seeing him star in an off-Broadway production of *A View from the Bridge*.

The veteran who owns a medical practice near your parents' house was once an extra in an episode of *M*A*S*H*, where he ironically did NOT play a soldier or a doctor.

At your coworker's birthday party, you wound up in a karaoke room with none other than Jaleel White. He was supernice, but refused to do the Urkel voice while duetting with you on Journey's "Separate Ways." The selfie you took with him was your profile picture on all social media for the next six years.

You once stumbled across the filming of a scene from a teen coming-of-age movie, starring some actors that looked familiar but made you feel old not knowing. When an assistant saw you staring and asked if you were an extra, you said yes, even though you were dressed for the gym, and the scene clearly took place at a prep school dance. You sat on a step in the background for two hours but have no idea if you made it into the final cut of the film, since you watched the trailer and it looked stupid.

While dining with friends at a gourmet pierogi restaurant, you spied Julia Louis-Dreyfus dining with two other women.

You spent the entire dinner pretending to listen to your friend's triathlon training stories while watching Julia out of the corner of your eye. On a trip to the bathroom, you passed by her table and worked up the courage to stop and say something. However, in a panic, you blanked on her entire filmography and blurted out, "You were great in *Troll!*"

While at the park near your apartment, you bumped into one of the dogs who played Marley in *Marley & Me*, and she was as nice in person as she looked on screen.

A New Patron's Guide to Sloppy Dave's Dive Bar

You seem like someone who's spent most of your life trying to hang with the cool kids. If you were at Tara Li's party, they were at Brian Swanson's party. If you were at the food court, they were by the sunglasses kiosk. If you were in Sara Lipton's basement watching her bat mitzvah video and playing *Saved by the Bell*: The Board Game, then they were, well, *literally anywhere else.*

You're in luck: As an adult living in the coolest city in the world, it's much easier to track down the in-crowd. They're inside clubs that have velvet ropes and forty-dollar cover charges. They're at rooftop bars sipping cocktails while gazing out at other rooftops bars. They're behind unmarked doors where they knew the bouncer, or their name was on a list.

But once you realize your name will never, ever be on that list, come on down to Sloppy Dave's Dive Bar.

Not to be confused with Fire in the Hole, the dive bar owned by your landlord, which has the logo of a gargoyle vomiting the signage, Sloppy Dave's is a local institution. It's the kind of place you may pass by, mistaking it for a bus depot. You pop inside and wonder, "Are the extras from *Pippin* having a cast party?" The bartender slides a drink in front of you, and you're at least 80 percent sure it's a beer? Possibly? Or a very watered-down whiskey?

The joint is filled with characters, like a low-budget Cheers, if Cheers was a halfway house for disenfranchised chimney sweeps. You may want to date Rolf, the toothless truck driver who wants to buy you a Heineken, but don't, even if it seems like a great way to stick it to your parents. Instead, banter with the bartender, an inattentive yet jovial sixty-year-old called Lucky, whose signature cocktail is a lukewarm can of PBR. Regulars include a set of flannel-clad buddies who live in the apartment next door and are responsible for the holes in the wall next to the dartboard (which were not caused by stray darts). There's JoEllen, a spindly towhead who, unlike the sash she is wearing, is not

"I forget—are we in line for the bathroom, or still waiting to get in to the club?"

in fact "Getting Married." She has a will-they-or-won't-they relationship with Rolf (as to whether or not they'll pay their tabs), and a penchant for drinking the ingredients of a tequila shot in the wrong order.

The only thing snazzier than the cast of characters is the atmosphere. The jukebox only plays the Steve Miller Band's greatest hits. You can never hear "Take the Money and Run" too many times, so bring lots of quarters. *Yes, quarters.* Cherry pepper string lights encircle the beer list, which is just a chalk drawing of an anatomically male bumblebee funneling from a keg. The seats smell like burnt hot dogs, despite there being no kitchen; the food menu consists of a bowl of hardened Swedish Fish on the bar.

Yes, there are no fewer than six bar patrons claiming to be the real Sloppy Dave, and all of them are strong candidates. Yes, the Christmas tree is still up, despite it being April, and also a fire hazard. And yes, the gummy floors try to suction your feet in place as if to say, "Rethink your decision to head to the bathroom here." This is the essence of Sloppy Dave's: cheesy, cheap, and inexplicably grim. So decrepit it's "cool."

You won't find a better dive outside of Tom Daley.

Casting Calls for the Role of "City"

Feature Film:
Sex & the City 5: And So It Keeps Going
Description:

Looking for a glamorous, ritzy background reminiscent of the late 1980s. Yellow cabs, Sardi's, and velvet ropes a plus. Should look like the inside of The Limelight, as designed by someone who's only heard it described to them by a much older friend.

Feature Film:
The Money-Launderer's Wife
Description:

Casting directors seeking settings for gritty period piece about mobsters, gangsters, and molls. 1920s–1940s, Lower East Side, NoLIta, Inwood. Would consider bridge-and-tunnel types.

Musical:
Broadway: The Musical
Description:

Casting a background for *Broadway: The Musical*, a musical-revue featuring songs from every musical ever made. Backgrounds should come prepared with their own marquees, billboards, and overpriced Italian restaurants. Auditioning cities should come brightly lit, stuffed with tourists, and include a dancing, life-sized Pikachu.

Feature Film:
The League of Majestic Marvels

Description:

Now casting the role of "City" in big-budget superhero epic. We are looking for a large metropolis, New York preferably, but will consider New York "types" (Chicago, San Francisco, Toronto, etc.). Must be able to perform its own stunts (collapsed bridges, crumbling skyscrapers, flipped cars). Experience with fire and explosives required.

Feature Film:
Off Duty

Description:

Looking for a city, late 1960s to early 1970s, for a film about police corruption in the ranks of the NYPD. Dark, moody, with sepia and gray overtones. Should be overcast and rainy, bleak, and slightly seedy. Picture a grungy Seattle-type, but with more dark alleys.

Scripted Television:
Law & Order: Bail Bonds

Description:

Casting cities of various locations to play the role of "City" in upcoming entry of *Law & Order* franchise. Potentially casting a Checks Cashed Here storefront, a Court of Appeals, and multiple jail extras. May use one location for multiple roles.

The Five People You Meet in Heaven, a New Club on the Lower East Side

Garvin: A bouncer who is as humorless as he is unflappable. Garvin will examine your license like he's searching for clues to the Holy Grail, and will spend ten minutes interrogating the male friends you came with, without ever letting any of them in. During the day, he's studying forensic science at John Jay College.

Janina: She's gyrating like she's trying to expel a snake from her tube top. Janina doesn't care if she's dancing on her own or not, but you can bet that if a circle forms, she'll be in the center. May have brought her own glow sticks.

Landon: He forgot his wallet—could you cover his entrance fee? And also his drinks? And the drinks of that blonde he's trying to go home with?

Elodie: She tagged along with some twenty-something coworkers, and she really wants to fit in. But, like, the music is kinda loud and repetitive, the strobe lights make it hard to see the drink list, and no one told her the wool turtleneck she wore to work wouldn't transition from day to night. You'll find her on a banquette in the back, sipping an espresso-tini and "guarding everyone's coats."

Carlos: Bartender on the main level. He can tell your age just by looking at your facial expression when he refuses to make you a White Russian. He totally sees you, by the way, but ignoring you is his way of letting you know the pile of singles you left on the bar could be a little higher.

Authentic

New York City: **long a popular tourist hub** for people from all over the world. But now that you've officially moved here, it's time to shed your young-ingenue-in-the-big-city schtick and act like you know which way Tenth Street runs (answer: on a bias). Here are tips for having a real NYC experience, from locals who've lived here long enough to know you're doing it wrong.

Best NYC Pizza

Hard-core pizza fans will tell you Roy's on Bleeker, Sal Mineo's, or House of the Rising Dough are the only ways to go. We agree – if you're willing to settle for a stale also-ran smothered in congealed toxic waste. If you want the best slice in the city, head to Pie Hard on Avenue D. It's the real deal; no toppings, cheese, sauce, fancy beverages, napkins, or plates to distract from the fresh-from-the-oven triangle slab scalding your palms with boiling grease. *Ahhhh,* New York!

Best NYC Nightlife Spot

If you like historic pubs and speakeasies, you'll feel right at home at Skivvies, a cocktail bar housed in the oldest functioning bordello in the city. Grab a private booth in the back–the cushions are repurposed from old sex cots. The red peeling wallpaper lends the space a seedy charm, and legend has it the bar was made from the tabletop where Sid "Knuckles" Stanley had a bullet removed from his thigh after a standoff with a madam. Order the Syphilltini, named after the venereal disease that wiped out half the crew of the SS *Barnacle* in 1927.

"We shouldn't have a problem getting in—
the bouncer's a buddy of mine."

Best NYC Hot Dog

Some native New Yorkers will try to convince you that Gray's Papaya is a thing, or to trek out to Brooklyn for a classic Nathan's Famous footlong. Those New Yorkers are lying: The minute you board an F train for Coney Island, they dash to the nearest vendor for a good ol' street dog. There is no more apt analogy for New York than a melting pot of processed meats squeezed together into a tiny tube, then marinated in a bath of its own filth for days. *Yum!*

Best NYC Theater Experience

Let the tourists flock to *Wicked* and *Phantom of the Opera*, *Shakespeare in the Park*, and the B-List Broadway on TKTS. You're ready for a true New York theater experience! Walk through Times Square to Eleventh Avenue and continue along the side of the highway until you see an abandoned gas station. Knock twice on the red door in the back of the convenience store. If a skinny bald guy named Randall answers, tell him I sent you and give him thirty-seven dollars in exact change. He'll give you a rubber Spiderman mask and lead you into a cubicle. You'll sit there in absolute darkness and silence for about an hour, then you'll hear soft whispering, followed by the piercing blast of glass shattering, and a woman screaming. Whatever you do, don't take off your mask. At this point, actors will come out and lead you from your cubicle into a small room. You'll stand there waiting for something to happen. Don't worry – this is all part of the performance. The room will start to fill with gasoline. When the gas rises to your chin, take off your mask and use it as a flotation device, then follow the lead actor and paddle your way out the door. You'll then watch a small vignette of actors pumping gas for cars coming off the West Side Highway, and . . . well, I don't want to spoil too much and ruin the magic.

Let's just say this is a step up from watching *Hamilton* without the original cast.

Best Place to Stay

Trust me, you don't want a cheesy tourist trap on the doorstep of the Empire State Building. Save bank and face by crashing in a NYC college dorm! Grab a sleeping bag from the lost and found and claim a space on the futon in the lounge, while a bunch of hungover sophomores binge-watch *Rick and Morty*. You'll get a taste of real city life, since everyone in the dorm definitely lives in NYC, at least for the rest of the semester. Nothing is more authentically New York than squashing a water bug with a stolen loofah in a communal shower.

Best NYC Restaurant

It's hard to narrow down the most authentic dining experiences in New York, but we have to go with Sharon's Place. It's *the* place to visit for a home-cooked meal that feels like you're eating in the home of an old acquaintance you haven't seen in years. Just ring the buzzer, ask for Sharon, and remind her you were in her sorority at Vassar. The restaurant only has one table, usually covered in Con Ed bills and mailers for local politicians, and the ambiance is best described as "casual casualness." Order the meatloaf, delicately coated in a layer of ketchup and frizzled onions, served with Birds Eye vegetables. Or try the stir-fry, heavy with the salty tang of excessive soy sauce. Or have whatever she's serving, since she only makes one meal, and is desperate for company. And maybe, if you're lucky, after dinner she'll show you photo albums from her semester abroad in Lisbon, and you can unwind while watching a *Late Show* rerun.

It's definitely BYOB; just make sure you don't bring the bottle Sharon brought to your housewarming.

Best NYC Spa

Empty your pores but not your wallet: Skip Bliss and head over to Bubbles Spa and Grill. Ask for Minty (her name might actually be "Mindy" and I just entered it in my phone wrong, but she's the best). Bubbles is known for its Red Velvet Mud Wrap, where you'll be slathered in terra cotta clay and cream cheese frosting. Your skin will absolutely glow.

Best NYC Comedy

. . . isn't found in a club. There's a group of drunk NYU grad bros who try unsuccessfully to skateboard in Union Square Park. It's hilarious.

"Well, this doesn't bode well for our life expectancy."

8

I COULD SELF-CARE LESS

A Timeline of What You Want the Vacant Storefront across the Street to Become

Day 1 in the City: An IKEA would be really helpful right now. That dresser you picked up outside your garbage room is looking kind of splintery.

Month 1: A fun cocktail lounge! Maybe a jazz club. A burlesque theater that also hosts spoken-word poetry slams.

Month 4: An entry-level workplace. When the highlight of your day is waiting less than ten minutes for all three of your trains, you may need a better job.

Month 6: This block really needs a fun, slightly upscale restaurant where you can get your Tinder dates to buy you spaghetti Bolognese and a bottle of Chianti before you tell them you're "not in the right headspace for anything more."

Month 7: A different urgent care center. The doctor at the one next door to your apartment has stopped prescribing Z-Paks for your head colds.

Month 10: OK, you know you asked for an Italian restaurant, but you weren't thinking of the Olive Garden. Maybe something . . . cuter? Where you can bring dates? Who aren't family?

Month 12: You're getting a little tired of the gourmet cupcake store around the corner, and the *other* gourmet cupcake place only takes cash, so the neighborhood could really use a fresh new cupcake joint, right?

Month 18: It would be great if that building became a gym, since you won't go if it's more than 10 yards from your apartment. Also, you've eaten a *lot* of gourmet cupcakes, so.

Month 23: Everyone in your building is so *young*. Where do they get their energy (and their edibles) from? Who's paying for their apartments? It would be cool if the building across the street was an apartment complex for, like, not-super-young-but-not-elderly residents who are looking to meet new people, but who play their music at a normal volume.

Month 28: A bicycle repair shop, since your front tire was stolen two weeks ago, as was your kickstand, seat, and the little bell you rang while trying to pass the dog walkers chilling in the bike lane.

Month 34: No judgments, but an L.L. Bean would be fantastic. Have you seen their new fleece hunting vests?

Month 36: A Bed Bath & Beyond, so you can return all the garbage you were pressured to put on your bridal registry and get that bread machine your carb-soaked heart craves.

Month 50: A clean, STEM-based playspace or daycare center.

"My purse didn't really go with this outfit."

The Stages of Getting a NYC Pedicure

Getting a pedicure is one of those weird luxury items where you pay a professional to do something that you could easily do yourself, like paint an accent wall in your apartment, or pluck your chin hairs. You'll try to spare the expense and do it yourself, but once you realize you have the body proportions of a T. rex, it's time to fork over the cash for someone else to groom your toenails. But whether it's your first or your one-hundredth pedicure, it's always the same deal.

Stage 1: Guilt

What kind of Queen of England move is this, paying someone to kneel in front of you and deal with the wreckage known as your feet? You should be out working in a soup kitchen or learning a foreign language.

Instead, you're reclining in a massage chair that feels like someone's tickling your lower back while wearing brass knuckles, with your feet submerged in mini Jacuzzis, *not* feeding the homeless or conjugating Portuguese verbs. You don't deserve this.

Stage 2: Insecurity

Why did you walk around in leather moccasins all day? Your feet smell like a gym mat after wrestling practice. Plus, your toes seem especially hairy today. Sure, this pedicurist has seen it all and worse. But still; that's a LOT of toe hair.

Stage 3: Confusion

You may have done this before, but you can't remember: Do you put both feet in the water? Now you take out one? Which one? Do you point your toes up or down? Are you supposed to look at the manicurist while she works? That seems pretty intense, but you want to show appreciation for her handiwork.

Stage 4: Blood-curdling Horror

GAAAAAH SHE'S FILING YOUR NAILS! What kind of squeaky-chalkboard/rubbing-cat-the-wrong-way agony is this???

Stage 5: Enjoyment

This woman is rubbing your feet. Your gross, stinky, hairy feet. Yes, you're paying her to do it, and yes, she's wearing a mask to keep a physical barrier between her oxygen and your grody insteps. But this is amazing. Give her anything she wants: money, insider stock tips, your firstborn, as long as she keeps kneading your heel with her delicate yet Navy SEAL–strong hands. *Ahhhhhhh.*

Stage 6: OCD

She missed a spot with the polish, right by the edge of your big toe. This is going to bother you. Should you say something? You can't stop looking at that missed spot. Also, you're pretty sure she rubbed your left foot much longer than your right foot. This will totally affect your equilibrium.

Stage 7: Boredom

You are literally watching paint dry. How long do you have to keep your feet under this dryer? Is it even on? Maybe you should touch the toe quickly to see if it's dry . . .

. . . Nope. And now you have a fingerprint embedded in your new pedicure.

Stage 8: Addiction

Look how shiny and mauve your toenails look! The underside of your foot feels like the wing of a newborn dove. Now you can wear open-toed shoes without looking like the "before" picture in a foot surgery ad. This . . . has . . . changed . . . your . . . life.

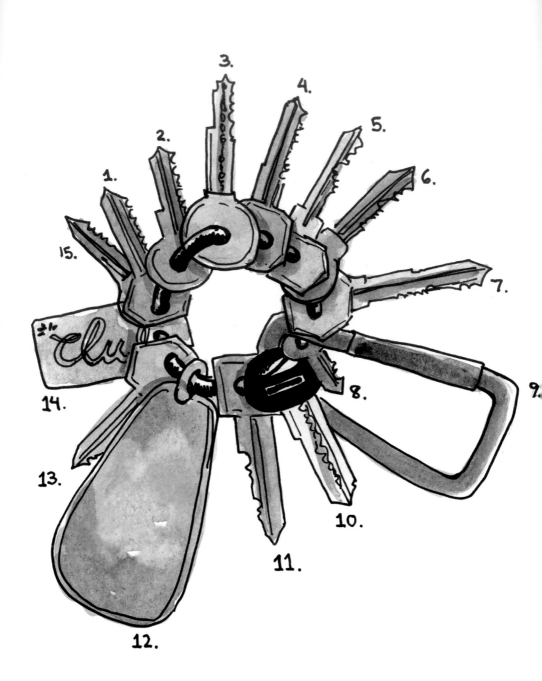

The Keys
You Carried

1. Key to the top lock of your apartment

2. Bottom lock. Righty tighty, lefty loosey?

3. Front door of your building, which is unnecessary, since the door never closes all the way

4. Replacement key you got after you left your keys at your parents' house during Thanksgiving

5. Key to deadbolt your mom insisted you install after your cousin's place in Philly was robbed

6. Replacement deadbolt key for when you locked yourself out of the apartment while doing laundry

7. Key to your parents' house that you keep for sentimental reasons, since all their locks have been replaced by entry codes and facial recognition software

8. Mailbox key. You should probably get the mail sometime.

9. Carabiner from that one time you went rock climbing for a bachelorette party, but you kept it because it makes you feel sporty

10. Key from the only car you've ever owned, a three-cylinder Toyota Tercel that was inexplicably stolen six weeks after you purchased it

11. Your neighbor's spare key that they left with you for emergencies, and also the only time you've ever seen that neighbor

12. Thanks for the stocking stuffer, Mom.

13. Key to your old office building, that you keep in case you need a bathroom in Midtown

14. FoodClub card that you keep forgetting to use, despite shopping in FoodClub every other day

15. Key to a safety deposit box in a post office on the edge of town, with instructions for your loved ones on what to do if you disappear for a while, along with the contents of your Swiss bank accounts

Times When You'll Really Love City Living

When you discover a free antique lamp left by the curb and it becomes the conversation piece of your living room for years to come.

When you stumble upon a free concert, like the bassist from REO Speedwagon performing in a Gramercy coffee shop, or a bunch of Broadway understudies belting out their shows' B sides in Bryant Park.

Right after it snows, and the city is coated in a dusting of glittery stillness.

When you get out of work after 11:00 p.m. and pass by not one, not two, but *eleven* options for takeout.

Turning down a small cobblestone street you never knew existed, then discovering a small uncrowded rooftop bar that just so happens to sell the rosé you fell in love with while wine tasting with your cousins in Montauk.

During the holiday season, when you brave the crowds of Rockefeller Center, make fun of the ice skaters who keep falling, watch the snowflake projections on a neighboring building, and stare upward marveling, "Jesus, that is a big goddamn tree."

Getting stuck under an awning in a thunderstorm with six other pedestrians, each of you waiting to see how much the rain has to let up before you make a dash for the subway.

Running late while meeting up with a friend, then sprinting right into a street fair, buying two mozzarepas (one for you and one for your friend), eating them both while browsing through the clothing racks, purchasing two ten-dollar pashminas (one for you and one for your friend), then deciding to keep both and to also stay for DJ Jammz's dance party by the Bank of America tent.

Finding three bars on the same block that all have jukeboxes with "Escape (The Piña Colada Song)," selecting the song five times, then exiting the bar quickly to the strains of "Yes I like piña coladas, and getting caught in the rain. . . ."

Bumping into your ex while you're holding hands with your new boyfriend outside a popular restaurant in TriBeCa.

All your trains arrive at the station just as you're getting there.

"One man's trash is another man's hostess gift."

9

A GIVING TREE GROWS IN BROOKLYN

Once there was a tree that grew between an abandoned shoe factory and a fish market, on a little up-and-coming industrial street in Bushwick.

And she loved a little boy.

And every day the boy would come

And he would shake her leaves onto the ground

And use them as a pillow while he napped

when he was supposed to be at school.

He would carve naughty words into her trunk

And drape his Vineyard Vines cardigan over her branches

And throw her apples at the bigger kids trying to steal his sneakers. The boy loved the tree almost as much as his Nintendo Switch. And the tree was happy.

But time went by, and the boy grew older. The abandoned shoe factory turned into an avant-garde art gallery, and the fish market became a tapas restaurant.

And the tree was often alone, surrounded by small fences designed to keep animals from defecating on her.

Then one day the boy came to the tree.

And the tree said, "Come climb my trunk and swing from my branches and eat apples and be happy."

The boy adjusted his knitted beanie and stroked his soul patch. "I'm taking a gap year before starting at my safety school, and I really need something to do."

The tree was perplexed. "I don't know what any of those words mean, but nothing passes time better than hanging out with your best friend, the tree."

"Actually, I've always wanted to open my own craft cidery on Sixth Avenue," said the boy.

"Take my apples, Boy, and buy a cider press and live your truth."

And so the boy had some of his buddies climb up the tree and gather her apples and carry them away.

And the tree was happy.

But the craft cider market was saturated, and the boy's investors pulled out, so he stayed away for a long time. . . .

And the tree was sad.

And then one day the boy came back, in tight pants adorned by unnecessary hemp suspenders.

The tree was now covered in posters for up-and-coming bands playing at the furniture store/hookah lounge that occupied the abandoned shoe factory. She trembled with joy. "Come, Boy, climb up my trunk and swing from my branches. No one's looking. It's not weird or anything."

"I am too busy writing my novel," said the boy. "I need someone to support me while I spend my days at Mr. Bean's Coffee hashing out my parent issues in a thinly guised erotic mystery set in Greenpoint."

The tree just kind of stared at him.

"Can you fund me via my Patreon page?" the boy asked.

The tree said, "I'm a tree, so I have no bank account, but you can cut off my branches and turn them into something you can sell. Then you will have money to finish writing." And the boy cut off her branches

And carried them away to whittle into miniature pan flutes to sell for exorbitant prices at the Brooklyn Flea.

And the tree was happy.

But the boy stayed away for a long time. The old fish market was now an artisanal ices shop that specialized in garlic-and-grapefruit sorbet.

And when he came back,

The tree shivered with the excitement of reliving the past.

"Come, Boy," she whispered, "come and play."

"I am a father now, to twin boys named Baden and Faden. My wife and I are looking for a nice place to eat brunch, then we're heading to IKEA to purchase a Bugaboo and a new apothecary table."

The tree was disappointed but said, "I don't know what any of those words mean, but you can cut down my trunk and make a table out of it. Then you can be happy."

And so the boy cut down her trunk and hired someone on TaskFinder to carve it into an apothecary table, and he, his wife, Baden and Faden ate gluten-free pancakes with huckleberry compote off it.

And the tree was happy . . . but not really. She missed the old neighborhood, and didn't understand why her block needed three vegan cupcake shops. She was confused by the boy's interests, and honestly, who would actually read a 1,000-page erotic novel about his parents?

And after a long time,

The boy came back again.

By now, the tree was surrounded by a small community garden share that provided antibiotic-free organic produce for the farm-to-table café operating out of the old fish market. The boy had more hair on his face than on the top of his head, and the tree wouldn't have recognized him if not for his tortoiseshell glasses and ironic T-shirt.

"I am sorry, Boy," sighed the tree, "but I have nothing left to give you —

My apples are gone."

"Cideries are passé – it's all about home-brewed cognac now," said the boy.

"My branches are gone," said the tree. "You can't swing on them – "

"I have bursitis in my joints and take herbal supplements just to be able to update my music blog," said the boy.

"My trunk is gone," said the tree. "You cannot climb – "

"This vintage Beetlejuice shirt actually cost $200 so I probably shouldn't get it dirty." The tree was at a loss.

"I don't need very much now," said the boy, "just a quiet place to sit and look at house listings on my phone. It's a buyer's market, and I could really use more space, so moving to the suburbs make sense."

"Well," said the tree, "an old stump is good for sitting and scrolling through Zillow. Come, Boy, sit and find your dream house in a good school district, near a Costco."

And the boy did.

And the tree was happy.

"See? This is why we need to move to a house in the suburbs."

10

I CAN SEE SUBURBIA FROM MY FIRE ESCAPE

Times When You'll Really Hate City Living

When you discover the free couch you pilfered from the curb was nesting a brigade of mice.

When you realize the expensive concert you've been eagerly awaiting is just a chance for your favorite artist to try out his new, much more depressing material.

About ten minutes after it snows, and the city is coated in a layer of cadaver-colored boot-printed sludge.

When you get out of work after 11:00 p.m. and pass by not one, not two, but *eleven* Columbia students who ask if you know where to buy weed.

Turning down a small cobblestone street you never knew existed, then discovering an overflowing dumpster that hasn't been emptied in more than a year.

During the holiday season, when you brave the crowds of Macy's trying to shop for your family, get trapped behind a line of ladies spraying perfume testers, impulse-buy a Timex for your dad because it already comes in a box, then see the checkout line wrapping around the entire floor and decide to buy everything online, like last year.

Getting stuck in Citi Field during a thunderstorm with six friends, none of whom thought to bring an umbrella despite all your phones predicting a "40 percent chance of precipitation."

Running late while meeting up with a friend, then getting stuck trying to cross Fifth Avenue during the Saint Patrick's Day Parade.

Finding three bars on the same block that all have juke-boxes blasting Billy Joel's "We Didn't Start the Fire."

Bumping into your ex while he's holding hands with his new girlfriend outside a restaurant you've been trying to get a reservation at for months.

Just missing your train, and the subway clock informs you it's 23 minutes until the next one.

"The pictures on Zillow made it look a lot bigger."

Are You Ready to Leave the City?

1. **During the summer, where do you spend most of your time?**

   A) Hitting up as many public parks as possible – did you know Prospect Park has horse trails?

   B) At work, earning enough overtime to go in on a house share in Hampton Bays with your college friends.

   C) Mooching off every suburban friend who has a pool and a barbecue.

2. **Where do you store your car?**

   A) Is this a trick question? You know where you'd store your horse. . . .

   B) In your Zipcar app.

   C) It's hard to parallel park a minivan in your neighborhood, so you keep it at your parents' house in New City, eagerly awaiting your return.

3. **There's another subway delay due to a signal malfunction. What do you do?**

A) Pull out your Kindle and dive back into *The Goldfinch*.

B) Text work to say you'll be late, then scroll through Vrbo looking for a weekend getaway.

C) Breathe the fresh air from your Zillow app to keep from hyperventilating.

4. **What do you want that vacant building across from work to be turned into?**

A) A new acai bowl lunch place.

B) A pocket park with a bench that's always vacant.

C) A new Long Island Rail Road station.

5. **When was the last time you had people over?**

A) One time you let the mail lady in to use the bathroom.

B) You let your cousins crash on your couch for a few days to thank them for lending you their lake house for Memorial Day weekend.

C) Your Thanksgiving dinner guests exceeded maximum capacity and all sorts of fire safety rules, but damn it, everyone loved your cranberry coulis!

6. What motivates you to leave your apartment?

A) Tickets to a new concert, show, club, or literary reading.

B) Your sister's wedding, but even then, only if there's an open bar.

C) A Con Ed worker dragging you from your living room because of a building-wide gas leak. Maybe.

7. The lady down the hall is:

A) Your best friend, whom you met when her fire alarm went off, and you bonded over your shared love of corgis. Come to think of it, *everyone* on the floor loves corgis.

B) Kind of nuts, but will leave you alone as long as you don't ask for your Amazon packages back.

C) Probably dead from natural causes, but that's none of your business.

8. When you hear how much your friend Maureen's new McMansion in South Carolina cost, you think:

A) "Yeah, but she has to live in South Carolina. *With Todd.*"

B) "How much for a summer rental in Myrtle Beach? We could be neighbors."

C) "That's half of what my sixth-floor walk-up studio with no windows costs!"

9. What sounds keep you up at night?

A) Ambulance sirens, shrieking strangers, and demolition are your white-noise machine.

B) Your mom, calling to see if you want her to pick you up from the Amtrak station for Aunt Lydia's birthday that weekend.

C) The faint ticking of the clock in your kitchen as it counts down the seconds until you vacate this cacophonous hovel.

10. What lawn tools do you already own?

A) Cornhole.

B) A plastic rake.

C) A cordless mulching mower, a riding lawn mower, and a woodchipper.

11. What type of flower is this?

A) A fake one.

B) A blue one.

C) A hydrangea macrophylla.

12. What do you love about your neighborhood?

A) It's full of cute restaurants, old-city charm, and it fits you like a fingerless Gore-Tex glove.

B) It's an affordable placeholder until you can move closer to work and friends.

C) If you squint from your window, you can see a tree three blocks away.

Answer Key:

Mostly As: Your heart and soul belong to the city. Good luck getting anyone from suburbia to visit you.

Mostly Bs: No need to move your car yet – there's still plenty of time left on your meter. But in keeping with the analogy, you need to hit the open road sometimes to keep the battery from dying.

Mostly Cs: Somewhere 100 miles outside the city is a small town, replete with strip mall, better schools, and an Applebee's, waiting for you to purchase a starter home. Go yonder, and regale the denizens with your gritty urban stories of surviving the Upper West Side.

"Ugh. Lousy Hamptons traffic."

50 Ways to Leave the City

The problem is your rental's small and priced too high

Your job's a joke, you're broke, your love life's DUI

Every day is just a struggle to get by

There must be fifty ways to leave the city.

You're sick of strangers who insist on being rude

Of paying large amounts for tiny plates of food

The crowds and smog and dirt will leave you in a mood

There must be fifty ways to leave your city

Fifty ways to leave the city.

You Irish goodbye, Ty

Ride on the tram, Graham

Pay for a Lyft, Cliff

L-I-double-R

Kosciuszko Bridge, Midge

Put your sofa in storage

Rent a Zipcar, Kumar

Your new home is far.

Ooh, get a new job, Rob

Find a new pad, Brad

Hop off the grid, Sid

It's time to move on

Google a route, Scout

Lincoln Tunnel your way out

Just picture your lawn, Shawn

And get yourself gone.

Your friends are sick of listening to you whine

About your lack of work-life balance all the time

Yet when your parents call, you say you're doing "fine"

But is there another way?

You fantasize of when you finally take flight

To a place with grass and trees and natural light

And zero pressure to be social every night

There must be fifty ways to leave the city

Fifty ways to leave the city.

You just slip on your bike, Mike

Find a "Man with a Van," Stan

Take a Jersey-bound ferry, Jerry

You can ride it for free

Pay a cab fare, Blair

Don't mess with a rideshare

Find a short flight, Dwight

And exit tonight.

Take the Amtrak, Jack

Rent a U-Haul, Saul

AirTrain JFK, Ray

From Terminal A

Chinatown bus, Gus

Get to Boston for not much

Just turn on your Waze, Hayes

And start your next phase.

"I can't tell if we're 'travel out-of-state for your birthday party' friends, or just 'hear about it afterwards' friends."

Don't Worry;
We'll Still Hang Out
All the Time

I know I'm moving out of the city, but it's just a short two-hour ride on Metro-North, then another quick jaunt down the 6 train to the 5, which is express, then a seventeen-minute walk to your place! Let me know when you all get together for drinks after work. If it's going to be an especially long hang, I can totally make it for the tail end. Last round's on me!

What's everyone up to this weekend? Does anyone want to grab dinner or see a movie? Maybe we can see if Seth's improv troupe is performing at The Lab. My schedule's really flexible – trains leave every hour, so I can meet you guys wherever you end up. Just give me a four-hour lead time, and a hint of what the dress code would be. This is going to be a blast! It'll be just like that time we crashed a rooftop soiree and partied with a minor-league hockey team until four in the morning. Except, this time, my last train leaves Grand Central at 11:26 p.m.

There's a new show opening on Broadway that I'm dying to see – a jukebox musical featuring the music of Steely Dan, called "Reelin' in the Years." It could be fun for all of us to get tickets. Maybe we could grab a bite beforehand near the theater. It's been a while since I've dined in the city; what are the hip trendy places in Times Square? I know there's an Olive Garden, *ha* (seriously though, their breadsticks are the bomb dot-com), but really, I'm down for anywhere, as long as

I can get chicken parm. So let me know what dates work for you. I'm free during all school vacations and can call Ticketmaster or whatever to get some primo seats.

Is Scott planning on throwing his epic New Year's Eve party this year? Count us in! Do you think he'll mind if we crash at his place? Six hours round trip for a party is tough, but we really want to see everyone. And you guys will get to meet our newest additions: Lilo and Stitch, our 200-pound mastiffs. I can't wait for all of us to ring in the new year together. Do you think Scott will be making his famous lemon-lime Jell-O shots? Never mind, we can bring our own.

Congrats on your new art show! It's a really big deal, getting to show your glass etchings in a fancy New York City gallery. And you can bet Tom and I will be there to celebrate your achievement. What time is your opening again? We can probably swing by after we pick up McKayla from day care. Maybe we'll even drive in! Do you think there's parking near the gallery? It's hard to parallel park our minivan, but McKayla has too much gear to drag into a ride share. Ugh, can you *believe* how much stuff toddlers need these days? Oh, I'm assuming the art show is interactive? And will there be juice and cookies, or just wine and cheese? Can't wait!

You guys need to come over and see our new place. It's a four-bedroom colonial on a quiet cul-de-sac, and each of us gets our own bathroom! Trust me, a lot of marital issues have been solved with this feature. We can barbecue in the backyard, and make sure to bring a bathing suit – we have an aboveground pool that Tom just put up, and all our rafts have drink holders, *ha ha*. When's a good day for you? We're pretty much free all summer, except for Justin's soccer tournament in Poughkeepsie, and McKayla's Tots-n-Toys camp, which runs from July through mid-August. But come on over!

Our house is a bit of a hike from public transport; do you have a car? Or can you borrow one? Do you want Tom to come down to the city to pick you guys up? He's been dying to get back to the old neighborhood. All he talks about is getting one of those massive slices at Chuckie's Pizza. Is Chuckie's still there? What about that video store that only carried Parker Posey films? I guess video stores aren't really a thing anymore. Has Parker Posey been in anything lately?

Well, if this summer doesn't work, there's always winter break. Or spring break. Or Memorial Day weekend, if you're not doing anything. Don't worry, we'll figure something out.

It's been too long.

That's Not How New York Does It

You're not my real city. OK, sure, I moved, but I'm actually a New Yorker. I plan on keeping my city address, even if I never receive another piece of mail again. I refuse to change my driver's license – this one traffic light town can't claim me! I never drove before coming here; I only showed my license when trying to get into fancy clubs or buying beer from FoodClub before 10:00 a.m. Now look at me, driving around, waiting until noon to buy beer, like an animal. I barely even recognize myself. I blame you, my stupid fake non-city.

You call yourself a city? Where is your cacophony of horns signaling that someone hasn't processed a green light fast enough? Where are your triple-parked livery cabs and your bike messengers driving the wrong way down a one-way street? Why is your public transportation clean and reliable? Honestly, if I wanted a quiet small-town life, I would've moved to Bedford Falls. But even George Bailey knew the real fun was to be had in Pottersville.

Why are all your bars closing at 1:00 a.m.? If I were in New York right now, I could walk into any building – an office, a laundromat, an ATM vestibule – and order a sidecar, and they'd slam it down in front of me with a bowl of olives and my folded towels. Now I have to go back to my apartment and drink the dregs of some gamey chardonnay that's been in my fridge for more than a month, and watch *The Late Show*, which is in New York, unlike me.

I know you're not New York, and I should just stop comparing you two, but still. New York has culture dripping from its pores. Do you offer any concerts that don't have the words *Winter* or *Jackson Middle School* before it? Speaking of shows, the Cinema 8 Multiplex does not a night out make. Where's your *Lion King*, your *Hamilton*, your *Wicked*? I have to settle for community productions of *Carousel*. If I wanted to see a bunch of schoolteachers warble "June Is Bustin' Out All Over" in a church basement, I would've attended my cousin's sad thirtieth birthday karaoke party.

You call this a variety of food? You have one Chinese takeout, one Italian joint that's basically just "pizza plus," and a barbecue place that's only ethnic if you consider "dry rub" a nationality. If I were in New York right now, I'd have a smorgasbord of options representing every land in the United Nations, including their territories. You can keep your upscale diners that feel like Michelin star restaurants; in New York, diners are dives on the periphery of town, greasy spoons with filthy utensils, waitresses putting themselves through sommelier school, and pie that's just "for show." That's how a real city does it.

Let's face it: New York City does it better, longer, grosser, and pricier. The bugs coming out of my bathtub drain are slimier, faster, and have more legs than the bugs anywhere else. The cost of a good exterminator is the same as one month's rent, plus utilities. The wait for booking an appointment with Roachy Rick is at least six months, at which point the bugs will have taken over my medicine cabinet and declared war on my cat. This is what I'll reminisce about as I sit on my porch and listen to cicadas boink.

I didn't want to move. I could've lived the rest of my existence in that 650 square foot pod of luxury. We could've raised our kids in the utility closet. They'd be worldly, cultured, independent, free-ranging around the West Side Highway like urbane chickens. Sure, they'd never hold a lacrosse stick, or experience the ease of attending a school simply because they lived near it. They'd never have a backyard, or a dog larger than a Yorkie. But Riverside Park would be their backyard. Their pets would be the peacocks that wander the food court at the Bronx Zoo. They'll take entrance exams to apply for pre-K, learn to duck under turnstiles, and grow to hate every single exhibit in Museum Mile, except maybe the Temple of Dendur, since it reminds them of *The Mummy* movies.

You can take the girl out of New York, but you can't take New York out of the girl, especially if she's had it implanted in her skin tissue by a tattoo artist on St. Mark's Place. I may not live there anymore, but New York will always be my city, my *real* city, and you will always pale by comparison.

Because nobody does it like New York.

Acknowledgments

I'd like to thank my parents, Marty and Marla Solomon, for regaling me with vivid descriptions of their childhoods in the Bronx (while being unable to recall what they ate for breakfast this morning). I was enticed by a world in which you knew everyone and everything, and could buy two slices of pizza and a soda for a quarter (and still get change back).

Thank you to my brothers Josh and Adam for hating NYC (something about "parallel parking on Queens Boulevard being the stuff nightmares are made of" or "this stupid MetroCard won't swipe"), but still visiting me anyway.

Thanks to all my city roommates over the years (Erin, Kristina, Nicole, Michelle, Joan, Kate, Shana, and a few randos) for creating fun times, removing all the full mousetraps while I curled up in the fetal position in terror, and watching millions of hours of *Law & Order* with me.

Thanks to my fantastic agent Rebecca Strauss from DeFiore Literary, for believing in this project, always going to bat for me, and sharing my love/hate relationship with all things NYC. And thanks to my terrific editor Brittany McInerney, and the rest of the Chronicle team (Maddy Wong, Jon Glick, and Alison Throckmorton), who had a vision for this project and helped me shape it into a beautiful product.

Special thanks to some of the fantastic editors I've worked with (Emma Allen, Chris Monks, Alex Baia) who have given my words and pictures a space to exist, have been extremely encouraging, and were the first to publish a few of the pieces from this book.

Thank you to David Getz, whose witty and poignant insights about his own life in NYC delight and inspire me every week. Thanks to Sienna and Violet, for being super city kids, seamlessly adjusting to the curveballs of the past few years, and allowing me to work at my own drafting table sometimes.

And most importantly, I'd like to thank my hilarious and supportive husband, Derek, for giving me the time and space to write/draw, providing endless encouragement during the dark parts, and being the ultimate gauge for whether something is funny. We've had a grand city adventure, and I'm excited for the next chapter with you.